I also am of Ireland

Frances Moffett

Frances Moffett left Ireland in 1924 never to return
there to live. She had contracted tuberculosis – at that
time a long-term illness for which little treatment was
available. When her own health improved somewhat she
remained in a sanatorium in England, teaching the child
patients, until 1932. She stayed in the teaching profes-
sion another four years, then trained for full-time work
in the Church of England, later becoming Vice-
Principal of a Women's Theological College. Retiring
from church work in 1960, she returned to teaching in
schools and a College of Education. Now, at the age of
84, she has put her own vivid memories of the years
before 1924 into *I also am of Ireland*.

I also am of IRELAND

Frances Moffett

'I am of Ireland
And the Holy Land of Ireland,
And time runs on,' cried she.
'Come out of charity,
Come dance with me in Ireland.'

W.B. Yeats

ARIEL BOOKS
BRITISH BROADCASTING CORPORATION

The BBC *Woman's Hour* serial based on this book was abridged
by Elizabeth Bradbury and produced by Pat McLoughlin

Cover illustration shows the Model School,
Galway, about 1913 with Frances (inset)
at the age of 18

First published 1985

Published by the British Broadcasting Corporation
35 Marylebone High Street, London W1M 4AA

Typeset by Phoenix Photosetting, Chatham
Printed in Great Britain by Mackays of Chatham Ltd

This book is set in 10/11 Ehrhardt Linotron

ISBN 0 563 20388 9

Contents

For Carol Burns
without whom this book would never
have taken shape

1900–5
'The House where I was born'

From the moment I woke up on that June day, I felt there was something strange about it. The curtains had not been drawn back. It was Bridget who came to get us dressed, 'us' being my younger sister, aged two and a half, and myself. I was exactly a year older.

'Hurry up, Miss Frances, get your things on. Everybody's very busy today.'

'Where's mother?'

'She's poorly.'

'What's wrong with her?'

'You'll find out. G'on – let you get those shoes on. What butter fingers you have! Come over here. It's time you learnt to button your own shoes.'

'It's my turn to have the dolly.'

'Here you are. Come on now. Down the stairs you go while I get the baby dressed.'

Slowly I began to go down the stairs from the top floor, clutching the big rag doll I shared with my sister. The shiny mahogany banisters looked very tempting. I loved to slide down them on my stomach, an activity which was strictly forbidden. There was no one about, so I slid down. As I got to the landing on the second floor, I came on my grandmother in whispered conversation with Dr Watson. He had a little black bag in one hand, his billycock hat in the other.

'It'll be a few hours yet,' I heard the doctor say.

'What'll be a few hours?'

Grandma saw me and gave the doctor a quick look, her finger on her lip. Fortunately, she had not noticed my way of descending the stairs.

'How would you like a new brother or sister?' asked the doctor. I didn't know the answer to that unexpected question, so just looked at him. He patted my head. 'You are growing into a big girl. I hope you're good.'

'On the whole, yes,' grandma answered for me. 'She is being a bit awkward over her food as usual.'

'I'll look in again in a couple of hours,' said the doctor, as he began to go down the stairs. 'Send for me if you think I'll be needed before then. So long.'

Just then, Bridget appeared with my sister in her arms.

'Bridget,' said grandma, 'as soon as the children have had their breakfast, take them for their walk. Keep them out as long as you can.'

'Yes, ma'am. It's a lovely day. Can I take them to Garbally?'

'It's a little far for Frances. But you can give her a lift in the pram if she gets too tired. You could take the little tin can with some milk in it, and a biscuit each – not more, or Frances won't eat her dinner.'

'I don't like milk.' This statement was ignored.

'All right ma'am. Do you want any messages on the way?'

'No, I think we've got everything.'

I felt very disappointed. I liked going into the shops. I was often given a biscuit or a sweet, after the assurance that I had been a good girl. In spite of my small appetite for rice pudding and vegetables and other things that were good for me, I was always ready for something sweet.

At first the walk was fun, for we went through the town across the Fair Green into Garbally Park. I knew it was where Lord Clancarty lived. We saw some red squirrels with bushy tails and some deer with their babies. Then Bridget met her soldier friend. He was very smart in his navy-blue jacket and trousers. There was a red stripe down each leg of his trousers. A pill-box hat was on the side of his head, kept in place by a strap under his chin. He had a cane tucked under his arm.

'You're not to tell your mammy we met me friend,' Bridget warned.

My sister Elizabeth went to sleep in the pram. I dragged on holding the handle of the pram which was made of twisted brass like barley sugar. The walk was much longer than usual and my legs got very tired.

'Can I have a ride? Grandma said so.'

'There isn't room with the baby asleep. You're getting too big for pram-riding now. There won't be any room for you anyway after today.'

'Why not?'

'Och, you'll find out soon enough,' said Bridget for the second time that day.

At last we got home. The house felt strange – everything was very quiet. Mother was nowhere to be seen. Grandma's parlour door stood open but she was not in her usual chair.

'Where's mother? Where's grandma?'

'They're having a rest. They were up half the night. You're to have your dinner in the kitchen.'

Dinner in the kitchen! I was sure my mother wouldn't like it.

'I'm not having my dinner in the kitchen!'

'Go hungry then,' said Bridget, as she took my sister down the long passage to the kitchen.

I stood at the bottom of the stairs feeling lost and lonely. Where was mother? I started to go up the stairs, running a little stick I had picked up in the park along the banisters. That at least made some noise.

On the second-floor landing there was a spare piano, shiny walnut wood with a green ruching across the front panel. I found that by stretching I could just touch the top. That gave me quite a thrill.

'Is that you, Frances? Come here.'

I heard my mother's voice from behind the partly-open door of the spare bedroom. I went in. There was mother in bed. She had on a lovely blue dressing-jacket, trimmed with wide lace. Her teeth were all stained brown.

'You're back from your walk. Come and look at your little brother.'

She drew back a shawl from a little bundle beside her in the bed. I looked down at the tiny, red, crinkled face, eyes tightly closed. I said nothing.

'Have you had your dinner?'

'No, Bridget said we were to have it in the kitchen.'

'That's quite all right. I told her to give it to you there. Now go down and get it.'

I went down, but not into the kitchen. I went into the garden. I was quite excited at what I had seen and heard.

A brother, I thought, a brother. He'll wear trousers. Trousers have pockets. Pockets have pennies in them. He'll give us pennies.

The house where I was born was large and roomy. It was built at the turn of the nineteenth century. Dunlo Street, Ballinasloe, County Galway was the address I was given in case I ever got lost. Next door was the Imperial Hotel, locally known as Kelly's. My mother and her five brothers had lived in the house from childhood. In it, four of my uncles died young; from it she was

9

married; to it she returned with my father. They had the upper part of the house.

The front door opened directly on to Dunlo Street. The hall was spacious; the oak stairs wide with shallow steps. Beside the stairs a long tiled passage led into a very large kitchen. Cooking was done on a coal range, kept shiny by polishing with blacklead. A row of bells connected to jars filled with sal ammoniac served the front door and several rooms in the house. Beneath the bells was a mahogany frame, to indicate which bell was connected to which room. On a shelf opposite the bells was a row of pewter ware, dishes, plates, tankards and goblets. They were just for ornament and never used.

My maternal grandparents had the two front rooms opening off the hall. One they used as a dining-room, the other as the parlour. The parlour was always welcoming; the fire glowing and warm. Either grandma or grandpa seemed to be there always, but especially grandpa. He was a Scot, over six feet tall, straight and slim. His neatly-trimmed beard and moustache were white, as was the thinning hair receding from his forehead. His eyes were blue and deepset. Two items of his dress never changed – the gold double watch chain, and the white linen handkerchief, a corner of which peeped from his breast pocket. I discovered that this handkerchief was only for ornament. To wipe his nose, grandpa took a large red handkerchief from his jacket pocket.

Two horsehair armchairs and a sofa to match were the main furnishings of the room; a large mahogany cupboard stood against one wall. In it were drinks for visitors, but more interesting to me was a silver-plated biscuit barrel. There is no doubt that grandpa spoilt me sometimes. Occasionally, the cupboard door was opened. Out came the biscuit barrel and I had a ginger biscuit; it was always ginger. One biscuit was enough to put me off my dinner, so sometimes I got a scolding, or rather grandpa did, in his absence.

'How often am I to tell your grandfather not to give you things to eat between meals,' mother complained.

I was a nuisance over my food. I had little appetite. I did not like things that were 'good for me', but I often longed for sweet stuff. I particularly disliked boiled eggs. I was sitting at a little table, a lightly-boiled egg in front of me.

'I don't want it,' I told Bridget.

'Doesn't matter what you want. You're having it. It's good for you.'

Suddenly Bridget pinched my nose with her fingers. I was

forced to open my mouth. The hated slimy egg was fed into me. As soon as Bridget released my nose, I was sick. I was given a couple of sharp smacks on my legs.

Meat I liked, but not green vegetables. It was the Sunday midday meal. I was on a visit to my paternal grandfather. He was carving the joint.

'I don't want any cabbage.'

'You've got to have some cabbage. It's good for you. You want to grow into a big strong girl, don't you?'

'Mn-n-mn.'

'Now, I tell you what I'll do. You see this nice piece of meat? I'm putting it on the side of the dish. When you've eaten all your cabbage and potatoes, you'll have it. Give her some potatoes and cabbage, Caroline.'

My aunt put some vegetables on a plate and passed it to me. 'What do you say?'

'Thank you.'

The meal went on. I toyed with the vegetables.

'Now Frances, hurry up. You're holding everyone up.'

Realising there was no reprieve, I began to push the vegetables into my mouth.

'Don't gobble! Is that the last bit? Good. Now pass up your plate and I'll give you your meat.'

'I don't want any meat now. I'm not hungry any longer.'

'Nonsense, child! There are starving children all over the world who would be thankful for this nice bit of meat! Pass up your plate at once.'

'I feel sick, I feel sick.'

'Whatever next! Up to bed with you until you learn to behave properly at table.'

'I never knew a child so capable of doing things at the wrong time,' said my mother. 'You even decided to be born in the middle of the October Fair.' It was my fourth birthday. I was in my grandparents' parlour, in the house where I was born.

Two large, low windows looked out on the street, crowded with animals and men. The view from one window was completely blocked by the backs of two gossoons seated on the window-sill. They had on bawneens of blue homespun. The cloth cap of one was so pushed to the back of his head that I thought it would fall off any minute. The other wore his cap at a jaunty angle.

'When are we going for our walk, Grandpa?'

'Oh indeed you'll not be going out while the Fair's on. You'd be trampled to death! Maybe your mammy'll take you to Toft's when the streets clear.'

That would be fun! Toft's brought a roundabout to the Green for the Fair.

There was a knock at the door. Bridget peeped in: 'Mr Bugloss to see you, sor.'

'Come in, come in, welcome! What'll you have? Whiskey?'

'Thanks.' Glass in hand, Mr Bugloss looked at me and patted my head.

'My, how you've grown. Can you read yet?'

'Oh, no she can't,' grandpa answered for me. 'She's not at school yet. Her mammy does a bit with her.'

'But I *can* read,' I protested.

'Get your book, then. You'll have a penny if you can read it.'

I ran upstairs and fetched the book. I opened it and pointed carefully to every word I read. 'Jack has got a cart. He can draw sand and clay in it.'

'Good girl,' said Mr Bugloss. He rummaged in his trouser pocket, brought out a handful of coins, selected a penny and gave it to me. Mr Bugloss went out. Soon after my mother came in. 'What's this I hear about Frances reading? She can't read a word.'

'Well, she's just read to Bugloss.'

'Show me what you read,' commanded mother.

I opened the book at the page and carefully pointed out the words once again.

'H'm,' was mother's comment. She took the book and opened it several pages on. 'Now, read that.'

Of course I was not able to. I had the other bit off by heart.

Mother turned to grandpa. 'I think it's safe to take them to Toft's. The streets have nearly cleared.'

My sister and I were taken up the hill and down the other side to the Fair Green. At the foot of the hill we met a man with a hurdy-gurdy. As he turned the handle it droned out, 'The wearing o' the green'. On the top of the hurdy-gurdy sat a grey monkey, dressed in a red coat, a red wollen cap with a tassel on its head. As we came along, it held out a tin can for halfpennies.

'Can I have a halfpenny for the monkey?'

'Me too,' said my sister.

Gingerly we went up to the monkey. He put out the paw holding the tin. When the money was put in the tin, the monkey saluted with its other paw.

In the middle of the Fair Green was Toft's roundabout. The sound of the organ was heard a mile away. Acetylene lamps made a big circle of bright light in the autumn dusk.

First we came to the caravans where the people belonging to Toft's lived. The caravans were gaily painted and decorated in green, blue and orange. The piebald horses that drew them were quietly grazing, each tethered by a rope to a stake in the ground. Beside each caravan a turf fire glowed. If a fire went dull, a lad fanned it into life again with a pair of leather bellows decorated with brass studs. Above every fire was a round, black, three-legged cooking pot, suspended from a tripod. Rabbit, potatoes and soda bread were being cooked in the pots.

'It'd be lovely to live in a caravan,' I said to mother.

'Maybe you'd think differently, if you did,' she replied.

The roundabout was playing, 'Goodbye Dolly, I must leave you', a song still popular from the days of the Boer War. On the roundabout were cocks painted bright green and yellow. There were horses, mottled grey with flowing manes. There were little cars with seats for the less brave. Above all, I wanted to ride on a cock. As the roundabout passed for the second time, I saw a lovely cock. It had long thin orange legs ending in orange toes, a bright red serrated cockscomb crowned its head, and the black painted eyes seemed to be looking at me. I watched for it as the roundabout slowed down.

'I want that cock there.'

'You'll go where the attendant puts you,' said mother firmly. I knew there was no arguing. The roundabout came to a standstill. My cock was exactly opposite us. To my delight, the attendant lifted me on to it. The music started again – it was 'A bicycle made for two' this time. But who wanted a bicycle to ride on when there was a cock?

The cock was very high. 'Hold on tight now,' said the attendant, his hand on my back. I grasped the little handle on the cock's neck. Up went the cock; down went the cock. All the time we were going round as well. The church, the convent, the trees of Garbally Park flashed by in turn.

The roundabout slowed down and stopped. The attendant lifted me down.

'Can we go again?'

'No, one ride only. It's long past your bedtime.'

We started the walk home. The unsold cattle were now in pens on the green: the cowherds were taking off their boots. Boots were a luxury, only to be worn on Sunday for Mass, or on some special occasion. They were tied together by the laces and slung round the owner's neck. He walked home barefooted, his feet hardened from childhood to the rough roads.

We paused, half-way up the hill, turned and looked down on the bright scene on the Fair Green.

'Well, you were born at a famous time, in a famous little town,' said mother. 'People come from as far as Russia for the October Fair.'

Perhaps being born in October was something I had not done at the wrong time after all.

The Fair week was the highlight of the year in Ballinasloe. It was talked about for weeks beforehand: it was the sole subject of conversation for weeks afterwards. How many foreigners had visited: how high were prices: was Toft's as good as usual? Then life settled down into its quiet routine. But it was not without its highlights for us. One was a visit of Uncle John from England. We children loved him. He had a big camera on a tripod. He took lots of photographs of us. The camera was a large box-like affair. Into it, when he was about to take a photograph, Uncle John put a dark glass plate in a wooden frame. He covered the camera with a long black cloth and disappeared under it for minutes on end. Every now and again he popped his head out from under the black cloth, and said: 'Peep-bo.'

It was the turn of Sam, the baby, to have his photograph taken. He was eighteen months old. Bridget brought him in. He had on a blue serge frock with puffed sleeves. Over the frock, he wore a stiffly-starched pinafore, gathered at the waist. It had cutwork frills at the neck, round the armholes and at the hem. He was barefooted.

Bridget seated Sam on a dining-chair. It had a shiny hollow oval back; the seat was of horsehair. Uncle John disappeared under his black cloth. In spite of an occasional 'Peep-bo', Sam got very restless.

'I want my horse! I want my horse!'

'Get his horse for him, please,' said mother. Bridget brought the horse. It was wooden, painted grey, with black hooves. It had a bent head and flowing mane. The horse was fixed to a small wooden platform with four wheels and could be pulled along by a piece of string.

For a minute or two there was quiet as Sam pulled his horse around the room. At last Uncle John was ready. Mother stood Sam on the chair so that he could see out of the window. He clutched his horse. Hopefully, Uncle John disappeared again under his black cloth. Sam's attention was attracted by the chimneys opposite. Black smoke came from most of them. He stood still. Then just as Uncle John pressed the rubber bulb that released the shutter on the camera, Sam shot up his right arm and shouted: 'Fire! Fire!' But Uncle John had got his photograph.

It was just before Christmas, 1905. My mother, my sister and I came to Miss Oliver's shop. It was a two-up two-down house in the main street which had been converted into a little toy-shop. The window, crammed with Christmas toys of every kind, was gay with silver tinsel streamers. Two stone steps led up to the door, which opened with a ping.

'Good afternoon,' said Miss Oliver. 'I got your message. I have saved two for you. They're selling fast.'

Miss Oliver went through a door at the back of the shop and came back with two black dolls. Each had a black woolly head and was dressed in a skimpy red-and-white striped garment. Miss Oliver gave one doll to my sister and offered the other one to me.

'I don't want a black doll.'

'You don't what?' said mother. 'Of course you'll have a black doll! Grandma's ordered them specially.'

'I don't want a black doll. It's not real.'

'Oh, what rubbish! Take it at once.'

'I won't, I won't! It's not real.'

'You are an ungrateful child. I'm sorry, Miss Oliver, about this. Come on now, take the doll.'

'I won't. I'd rather have a book.'

'Well, you can't have a book. You have the black doll or nothing – make up your mind.'

'I won't have it. It's not real.'

'You're behaving disgracefully. Now once and for all, are you going to take that doll.'

'No. It's not real.'

'All right then. Go without.'

I left the shop empty-handed. I was beginning to learn a lesson of life. It was not what I wished but what grown-ups wished that mattered.

1905–6
Life in Ballinasloe

Each year in Ballinasloe, there was a big social event – the Hunt Ball. From all the surrounding villages and estates, the upper stratum of society drove into Ballinasloe in horse-drawn vehicles. The ladies needed somewhere to rest and change. Our house was, by long custom, one such place. It had something not yet common in the West of Ireland, a bathroom and a water closet. We were allowed to stand on the upper landing and peep through the banisters as the ladies came through the hall. All wore rich satin or brocade evening gowns. Occasionally a diamond necklace glinted as it was caught in the gaslight. Several of the ladies had ostrich feathers in elaborately dressed hair. Bridget stood in the front hall. She had on her afternoon black, her prettiest white lawn apron, and an embroidered cotton cap with long streamers. As a lady came down the wide stairs, Bridget helped her to put on her long evening cloak. There was always a discreet movement towards Bridget's hand.

'Bridget does very well out of the ball,' I heard mother say. I wondered what she meant.

'Are you going to the ball, mother?'

'Dear me, no! We're not high society!'

I was beginning to be dimly aware of the distinctions in class. There was high society; there was us; there was Bridget and my grandfather's men. My father was a veterinary surgeon. My mother had been a teacher before her marriage and, according to the marriage certificate, my maternal grandfather was in the plumbing and gas-fitting business.

'Where are we going for our walk today?' Not a day passed but this question was asked. The walk was the exciting event of the day. A lot depended on who took us out. Usually it was Bridget. Bridget was always told where we were to go, but she did not always keep to her instructions. She liked to call in at the chapel. Now Bridget was a Roman Catholic: we were Protestants.

Between the two forms of worship there was a great gulf fixed. Catholics were not allowed to go into a Protestant church: Protestants seldom chose to go into the Catholic chapel, for them the symbol of error and superstition.

'Now ye won't tell yer mammy, if we go into the chapel, will you?' We promised, for the chapel was exciting. It was large, dark and mysterious, with glowing stained-glass windows, so different from the whitewashed, plain-windowed building we went to on Sunday. The chapel was full of interesting things. Just inside the door was a statue of Jesus as a young man with a lamb in his arms; above it a large plaster cast of a bleeding heart. 'That's the sacred heart of Jesus,' Bridget told us. I could not bear to look at it. The Virgin Mary had the place of honour on the right-hand side of the sanctuary. She stood on a high plinth, tall and regal. Her gown was white, half-covered by a blue drape. On her head there gleamed in the half-light a crown of gold. 'The crown's to show she's the Queen of Heaven.' Bridget used to cross herself with water from a little basin at the church door, 'to keep away the Devil'. Then she put a farthing in the little box and lit a candle.

'It's to ask St Jude to find me ring for me,' she explained. The candle was added to the dozens already burning on an iron stand. 'They're all the prayers going up to the saints.' Bridget was a born teacher.

As the candle flames danced in the darkness from the light breeze that came through the chapel door, which always stood open, it was easy for a child to take Bridget at her word. But for me such a visit was spoilt by the feeling of guilt that we had been on forbidden ground, and must not say anything about it.

One day Bridget took us into the convent. This time it was to take some toys from my mother 'for the orphans'. Once a year, just before Christmas, we were taken to the orphans' Christmas tree. While we lived in Ballinasloe, we did not have a Christmas tree at home. I imagine my Scottish Presbyterian grandfather considered it 'pagan and Roman Catholic'.

The convent was entered by a solid wooden gate from the main street. In the door was a square shuttered grille. On the right-hand door plinth was a highly-polished brass knob. When the knob was pulled, a bell clanged inside.

'I can reach to pull the bell. Can I?'

'Yes,' said Bridget. I pulled the knob hard.

The grille shutter was shot back and the face of Sister Philomena appeared. It looked rosy and chubby in its surround of a winged headdress of black and white.

'An' is it yourself, Bridget? An' how are you?'

'Very well, Sister. The missus has sent some toys for the Christmas tree.'

'How kind of her, now. Come on in.'

The big door swung open and we went in. As the door closed the outside world seemed to be shut out. All was peace and quietness.

'Go straight up to the front door.' The sister went back into a little porter's lodge by the gate. The path to the convent front door had a row of smooth round stones on each side. They bordered lovely lawns. Wallflowers had been planted in the flower-beds, to become cushions of red and yellow in the spring.

'D'ye see that stone?' said Bridget pointing to one. 'That is where the voice came from.'

'What voice?'

'Ye won't tell yer Mammy, if I tell you?'

I promised.

'Well,' said Bridget, 'one day I came to Mass in the convent here. I hadn't been to Confession. Yer Mammy had let me out, but I met my soldier friend, and got too late. You know it's a mortal sin to go to Communion without having been to Confession, so when the priest put the Host on my tongue, I was afraid to swallow it. I kept it in my hand until the Mass was ended. Then I put it under that stone. In the evening I was going to Benediction. As I passed the stone, I heard a voice calling "Bridget, don't leave me here". I was scared out of my wits. But when I lifted the stone, the Host was gone.'

For days afterwards, every time I passed a big stone I expected to hear a voice. I had promised not to tell my mother and didn't. But my aunt, a strict Presbyterian, came to stay. She took us for a walk. As we passed the convent, I couldn't help telling her about the voice in the garden.

'I've never heard such superstition in my life,' she said. 'It's a lot of Roman Catholic nonsense.'

I think something was said to Bridget, for the visits to the chapel ceased.

Another day, we were out for a walk with grandpa. We had got as far as the Asylum. A ten-foot-high limestone wall hid the building. The way in was through a black iron gate, always locked.

Suddenly down the road came a sidecar at full speed. It had two seats back to back, the driver on a seat in front, urging on his grey horse. On one seat was a girl screaming. She had a long brown skirt: a black shawl round her shoulders clutched in both hands. Her bright red hair flowed over her shoulders. She struggled and kicked. On each side of her was a policeman holding her by the arms.

'She's mad, poor girl,' said grandpa.

'Holy Mother of God, save me, save me,' she kept screaming.

The big iron gates were opened by a man with an enormous key. The girl, her red hair streaming behind her, was dragged inside the gates. They closed. We went on.

'Now you two, go out into the garden. Don't get those clean pinafores dirtier than you can help!'

Mother was tying the tapes on the backs of the pinafores on my sister Elizabeth and myself. They covered calf-length blue serge frocks. Each pinafore of stiffly-starched cotton had a broderie anglaise frill round the neck. Stiff frills decorated each armhole. Another trimmed the hem, which often had two or three tucks above it. These were let down as a child grew.

Though our house was in the centre of the town, it had quite a large garden. The stone walls were covered in ivy. There were a few apple trees on a stretch of grass. My father grew some vegetables in a plot at the far end. Peas did well, and among the local residents there was considerable competition to get the best peas for the flower show. Our garden adjoined that of Kelly's Hotel: Mr Kelly also grew peas. He had three sons, one of whom, Andy, was just a year older than me. We went into the garden. Over the wall Andy's head appeared. He had a fistful of peas.

'Would you like some?'

'Please.'

He threw down the peas. The small new peas were tender and sweet. I don't know how many we ate, but before long, my stomach, always tricky, began to reject the raw vegetable. I was violently sick. The reason became obvious.

'Have you been picking your father's prize peas?'

'No – no.'

'Where did you get them, then?'

'Andy gave them.'

'You should have known better than take things from Andy. Now get off upstairs to bed.'

Poor Andy! He did not get off so lightly. The peas he had given us were also his father's prize peas. He got the slipper, but bore me no ill-will for unintentionally giving him away.

Not long after, I collided with him in the street, as he was running down to the chapel. I was rushing back from the next-door shop where I had been sent for a message. His front tooth broke in my forehead. I still have the scar.

There was not a great deal to do in the garden. Skipping soon became boring. Balls were forbidden because of the windows. At the back end of the garden there were two sheds. No one had actually forbidden us to go into these sheds. The bolts were high up but I was growing into a tall child. One day I was in the garden on my own. I could just reach the bolt of the nearer shed, it moved easily and the door swung open. Bright sunshine showed what was inside. I was filled with horror and fear. Hanging from two lines across the shed were the entrails of animals – all bloody. There were livers, hearts and intestines. It was the place where my father carried out post-mortems and research on animals that had died. I think that occasion was the beginning of a phobia about blood which has dogged me all my life.

Another day, Elizabeth and I were sent into the garden with our doll. It was about two feet high with a round, moon-like face, bright red-painted cheeks and bright blue eyes. On it was a baby's cast-off frock. The doll had come from *Weldon's Ladies Journal* as a flat piece of material, with the outline of the doll painted on it. Mother had cut it out, sewn it up and stuffed it with cotton wool. We had to share it. I never remember any quarrels over it, probably because I usually preferred a book.

The door of the other shed stood open as the inside had been freshly scrubbed. It was the clay privy for the men who worked about the place.

'The dolly wants to do number one,' said my sister.

In we went. There was a high wooden seat with a hole in the centre. We set the doll up on the edge of the hole. She toppled over and fell into the smelly morass below.

'I'll get her.'

I was about four and not much taller than the seat. However, helped by my sister, I scrambled on to the seat, leant over the hole and tried to get the doll. The hole was larger than I was, and suddenly I was suspended head down in the dark. I held on to the side of the hole, but could feel myself slipping when I tried to move.

'She had great common sense,' said my mother later to my grandmother. She was referring to Elizabeth. 'She came toddling into the kitchen, and tugging at my apron tried to tell me something. I realised something was the matter. "Show me," I said. She trotted up the garden to the privy. We could just see Frances's legs. We pulled her out, frightened, but none the worse. It'll be a lesson to her.'

Behind the garden were the stables. Next to the house was an archway with a green wooden gate. The stables were reached through this gate.

We had one grey mare called Dolly Grey. She was born during the Boer War and named from the famous song of the time. My father drove this mare in a gig to a case, if the distance was not too far. Sometimes he hired another horse to give Dolly Grey a rest if he had been particularly busy.

As well as a gig, we had a little pony trap. It was of pine-coloured slatted wood, with large wheels and scarlet cushions. Mother used to drive the pony trap.

It was the local Agricultural Show. Mother was the only woman to enter for the best pony and trap. Very upright, she looked smart in her grey costume and toque. A black veil covered her face. She drove the pony and trap three times round the course on the Fair Green. Then she joined the other competitors drawn up in a ring. The judges went round and made notes.

Then came the awards. The first, second and third prizes went to two well-known local men.

'As we have a lady in the event, we are awarding a special consolation prize for a very neat turn-out,' said the chief judge. A white rosette was pinned on Dolly Grey's halter.

'I don't like it at all,' I heard my mother say to my father. 'They've only given me that prize because I am a woman.'

She was a keen feminist.

'I'm afraid that is so,' replied my father. 'Dolly Grey'll never win a prize at a show. She doesn't lift her feet. Only high steppers have a chance.'

'Well, it's touch and go,' said Doctor Watson, as he took up his billycock hat and little Gladstone bag.

'Keep him as warm as you can. See if you can get him to take a little peptonised milk. I'll come again later on.' The doctor went out with my father.

Mother was sitting in a low rocking chair. She wore a white, high-necked blouse, fastened at the throat by her everyday brooch. It was a silver Celtic knot, with a blue-grey stone in the centre. Her dark hair was already greying at the temples – the greyness shown up by the false puffs over which her hair was brushed. Her long dark skirt was partly covered by a small woollen blanket. On her lap lay a scrap of humanity, her younger son, three months old. His tiny face was wizened and bluish. Occasionally, he whimpered. Mother caressed the damp hair on the baby's forehead. The diamonds in her engagement ring flashed now and again as they caught the flickering firelight.

A turf fire was burning in the black grate. A neat stack of turf sods was piled in the hearth. On a brass tripod in front of the fire there was a black enamel saucepan, filled with hot water. In it was a baby's boat-shaped glass feeding bottle. It rested against the rim of the saucepan, the rubber teat just visible.

Beside the rocking-chair was a small bamboo table. A bronze bronchitis kettle heated by a spirit lamp stood on it. From its long spout, there came a continuous gush of steam. The smell of camphorated oil seemed to fill the room.

No one spoke, or said anything to my sister and myself, perched on chairs and, for once, quiet. The silence seemed filled with foreboding – broken only by the baby's choking wheezing, and my mother's occasional, 'There, there.' There were footsteps on the stairs. My father came back.

'I've sent a telegram,' he said. 'I won't go to my Loughrea surgery. Dr Watson says the crisis will be before the evening.'

My sister and I were put to bed for the afternoon. At teatime, grandma came to wake us up. She took us downstairs. Dr Watson was coming out of the sitting-room.

'How's the baby?' asked grandma.

'Good news. He's taken a turn for the better. With a bit of careful nursing, he ought to be all right now. I'll probably have a look in last thing.'

There was a feeling of relief in the sitting-room. The fire was burning brightly. My father was just going out on a case. The baby was taking his bottle. There was jam for tea even though it was not Sunday.

1906–8
New Experiences

'I'm not sure whether they're old enough for this sort of thing.' My mother was looking at some tickets she was being offered. 'Still, they have to begin sometime. I'll take one ticket and two halves. I see it's at three o'clock on Thursday.'

'Where are we going on Thursday?'

'To a Conversazione.'

Conversazione. What a lovely word. I rolled it round on my tongue.

'What do we do there?'

'Well – listen to music and recitations and have tea.'

It sounded quite exciting. Thursday came. The Conversazione was evidently an important occasion. Mother had on her strawberry cloth coat and skirt. The skirt was ankle-length and gored, the jacket short and closely fitted to her neat waist. The lapels, in velvet, were of deeper strawberry. On her head she had a natural straw toque with ribbon bows to match the suit.

My sister and I had on our best pelisses. They were coats of pale grey cashmere, with deep round cape-like collars, embroidered in cream. Our maiden aunts had sent them. We were the only nieces.

'Not very practical,' mother had commented, so they were kept for special occasions. Our bonnets, lined with cream silk, matched the pelisses. Open-worked lace gloves completed our costumes. The gloves were a handicap. I got into much trouble for picking lichen off the stone wall while wearing them. The lichen left a green stain which proved indelible.

Sedately we walked down to Mrs Rossiter's. A maid with flowing streamers from her cap showed us into the drawing-room. There were about a dozen ladies there, but no other children. We sat on straight chairs. For some time the ladies chatted.

'Of course you know about . . . ?'

'It's high time something was done about the gaslight . . .'

'They say she's . . .' Finger on her lips from my mother interrupted this.

'I think it's time to begin.' Mrs Rossiter, our hostess, opened the grand piano.

Then there began what seemed interminable boredom. Someone recited Portia's speech from the *Merchant of Venice*. It was much applauded. Another lady played 'The Robin's Return' on the piano. It was interesting to watch for the moments when she crossed her left hand over her right. Recitation followed recitation: classical song followed classical song. Mendelssohn's 'Songs without Words' seemed endless.

'Sit still: stop fidgeting,' came at intervals in a whisper from mother.

But at last there came some light relief. Two diminutive ladies stood up amid great applause to sing a duet. They were the Misses Bellew, local celebrities. They looked like twins. Each wore an identical brown silk frock with long full skirt, the high necks of the bodices held stiff by little whalebones, the fronts trimmed with handmade tucks and real lace. The sleeves, puffed at the shoulder line, looked like little hills. The Misses Bellew stood side by side next to the piano. Each held a small slip of paper in her right hand which was crossed over the left.

'Rock of ages, cleft for me,' sang Miss Gladys in a high-pitched treble voice.

'Rock of ages, cleft for me,' echoed Miss Violet in a deep contralto.

'Let me hide myself in thee,' Miss Gladys, high up.

'Myself in thee,' Miss Violet low down.

It was too funny to resist. Giggles took over. Disapproving glances came our way. Mother looked at us and shook her head.

Loud applause greeted the end of the duet, and the cultural part of the Conversazione was over. Mrs Rossiter pulled a coloured rope by the window. The maid with the long streamers came in carrying a silver-plated tea tray. On it was a silver-plated teapot, and a silver-plated kettle with a spirit lamp under it. She took off a shower cloth from a table in the corner. Mrs Rossiter's best Crown Derby china was displayed in all its glory. It had a design of russet red, royal blue and gold.

The maid reappeared with a large four-tiered wicker cake-stand. One tier had a Crown Derby plate of tiny cucumber sandwiches on a frilly doily; another had scones; another a fruit cake, while on the bottom tier was one of Mrs Rossiter's raspberry sponges for which she was famous!

While Mrs Rossiter presided at the teapot, the ladies drew off their kid gloves, smoothed them neatly and laid them on their laps. Then each balanced a delicate cup and saucer in one hand, while eating a tiny sandwich with the other. No plates were provided, as it was afternoon tea. Food rested in the saucer. It was genteel to turn up the little finger of the right hand, while drinking from the cup.

'I've something special for the children,' said Mrs Rossiter. 'Mary's just bringing it in.'

In came Mary with two glasses of milk and two Marie biscuits. I hated milk, but with mother's eye on me I managed to gulp it down.

It was my first and last Conversazione. When we got home I went into my grandfather's parlour. He always had a willing ear.

'Did you enjoy the Conversazione?'

'It was very funny.'

'Very funny?'

'Yes, the Miss Bellews sang "Rock of Ages".' I began to mimic them, trying to sing high, then low. My grandfather was horrified.

'It's religious,' he said. 'You must never mock religious things.'

'I wish I were good-looking,' I thought, 'then I mightn't be thrashed.'

I was looking at myself in a mirror. I knew I was plain. My sister was very nice-looking. She had a madonna-like oval face, dark brown eyes, and shining black hair. Her good looks seemed to bring her definite advantages. 'What a lovely-looking little girl,' people said. I don't think I was jealous of her. I took my own plain looks for granted. Indeed, I felt a certain reflected glory in being the sister of a beauty.

'Wait until you get to school my girl,' had been said to me more than once. Now the day had arrived. I was going to school for the first time. I was nearly seven, but in Ireland there was no compulsory education act. My mother, herself a teacher, had taught me at home. My picture of school came from *Tom Brown's Schooldays* which my mother had been reading to us. It seemed that thrashing was part of school life and inevitable. I hoped I would have the courage not to cry.

'Now are you ready? Have you got your shoe bags?'

We set off with mother to walk the half-mile to the little school in Mount Pleasant Avenue. There it was – a small, solid whitewashed building, set in an avenue of ash trees, overlooking the Fair Green. I had passed it many times on our walks – it was just the school. Now it was something very different. As we went through the porch into the large single room, I had a sense of adventure mixed with dread of what was to come.

At one end of the room was a large window pointed at the top, just like the window in the church. A coal fire blazed in the black grate. Round it was a shining brass fireguard about three feet high. Ten brown desks were arranged in two rows. There was a shelf for books under each desk. Pottery inkwells, freshly filled with black ink, had round shining brass covers. The children sat on benches without backs.

The teacher had a tall desk with a lid that lifted up. We never saw inside it. On the desk was a small cane, and a clock in a black ebony case. The big clock on the wall did not work. It had stopped at five to one. The floorboards were bare, but well-scrubbed, and smelt of carbolic.

The teacher came to the door to meet us.

'Good morning, Miss Corfield,' said mother. 'Here are the girls. They can find their own way home across the green. I'll send Bridget to meet them.'

Mother left. There were no goodbyes or kissing in those days. Miss Corfield was tall and thin. She wore a long black skirt, and a white shirt blouse with a high starched collar. Her abundant dark hair was scraped back into a bun on top of her head. From a wide black leather belt there dangled a bunch of keys.

'Here is your peg,' said Miss Corfield, taking us to a row of pegs in one corner of the room. 'Take off your boots and put on your slippers. Then hang your slipper bag on your peg. Come here, Frances, your hair ribbon's slipping.' She retied the blue ribbon very tightly on my fine untidy hair. It hurt all day.

'Scripture first,' she said.

The school was what today would be called 'independent'. It was financed and run by the Presbyterian Church for the small Protestant minority in the town.

Scripture began. We stood in straight rows, the youngest in front. As it was the first day of school, we had Psalm one in the metrical version. Miss Corfield said the words line by line.

'That man hath perfect blessedness,' she said.

'That man hath perfect blessedness,' we chanted.

When we were word-perfect, we learnt the tune. Miss Corfield then went to a harmonium and we sang the Psalm. The words and tune are still with me . . .

'That man hath perfect blessedness
That walketh not astray
In counsel of ungodly men
Nor stands in sinners' way
He shall be like a tree that hath
Been planted by a river,
Which in its season bears its fruit,
And its leaf fadeth never.'

As we sang, in my mind's eye I saw the evergreen trees which grew along the banks of the little local river. Each tree was topped by a man's head.

After scripture, came geography. I'd never heard the word, but acquired a very interesting bit of information.

'You must build a house on the side of a hill,' said Miss Corfield, 'so that the water runs away. Then there will not be any danger of flooding.' She went to the blackboard and drew a square house on a slope.

The highlight of that first school day was 'spelling'. About ten of us were arranged in a semicircle. As the newest pupil, I was at one end of the semicircle. The teacher called out a word and, most mysteriously to me, the children began to change places. I couldn't make out why they were doing this. No one suggested I should move, so I remained where I was. Then an extraordinary thing happened.

'Spell "message",' said the teacher. One child after another failed to spell the word.

'Wrong,' she said. At last she came to me.

'Can you spell "message"?' Well, at least I could do that. My mother was very strict about spelling.

'M-e-double s-a-g-e,' I spelt. There was a gasp of surprise from the teacher. It did not equal mine when I was pushed from one end of the semicircle to the other, still not understanding why.

The first day of school was over. I had not been thrashed. I had even been called, 'good girl'. I had lots of new information to pour out in triumph, when I got home. I told my grandfather about the gymnastics in the semicircle. Apparently, I had done something praiseworthy in just spelling a word. My grandfather gave me a penny.

School was a lovely place. I determined to be a teacher when I grew up. From that determination I never wavered.

My mother came into the spare bedroom, carrying a small red paraffin lamp. 'Now you two, get off to sleep. You have to be up early in the morning,' she said as she blew out the candle on the mantelpiece. She went out and closed the door.

Sleep did not come for my sister and myself. Unusually, we were in a double bed with a feather mattress. It was soft and bouncy, unlike the bed-board on which I usually slept.

'Let's make up some poetry,' I said. I liked making up poetry, but it never impressed my mother.

'You can't call that poetry,' she would say, but never explained why. The muse was active: the poetry came.

'Hurrah, hurrah, for tomorrow
In Gentian Hill we'll be:
Hurrah, hurrah, for tomorrow,
Digging by the sea.'

My sister, more musical than I, found a tune, and we began to chant the jingle.

The door opened: my mother looked in. 'Stop that row at once, and get off to sleep. I won't tell you again.' The door closed firmly.

It was our last night in the house in which we had been born. We were very excited. Next day we were to move to Galway, a town on the west sea coast. I had never seen the sea. In my imagination, I saw a large concrete basin full of water like the ornamental pool in Garbally Park.

There had been upheaval for days. Articles of furniture and tea chests of china and other belongings had been taken to the station on a large horse-drawn dray. These had gone ahead in a furniture wagon attached to the mail train.

Morning came. It was 18 December 1908. We got up, washed and dressed, had breakfast all in a hurry and waited in the hall for Kelly's bus. This was a black, oblong, box-like vehicle which went between the station and the Hotel. It could carry about ten people, and had wooden seats on either side. Grandma and grandpa were in the hall with us. The bus came on time: we four children were put inside. I, the eldest, was just eight: the youngest, a brother, Alec, was two and a half. Elizabeth, always the maternally-minded one, clutched our rag doll.

A few neighbours came out to see us off. Goodbyes were said. The bus, horse-drawn, trundled down Dunlo Street, turned left into Society Street, and rattled along on its iron wheels for the Irish half-mile to the station.

We were the only passengers for Galway. The station-master, distinguished by his frock-coat and small peaked hat, came out to greet my mother. The signal went down with a loud click. In the distance the black engine appeared round the bend. Red sparks, mingled with thick black smoke, came from its funnel. Chunk-akan, chunk-akan, chunk-CHUNK-AKAN got louder and louder. As it drew nearer, I crouched back against the wall, afraid in case the black monster should leave its rails and mount the platform. The train slowed up as it entered the station and came to a halt with a long grunt from its brakes. The station-master opened the door of a first-class carriage, as was his privilege, and we climbed in. The trunks were put in the luggage van. Two wicker baskets and a black Gladstone bag were put on the rack in the carriage. Rugs were tucked round us, as there was no heating in the train.

The station-master shook my mother's hand. 'We'll miss you all,' he said, 'but himself's right to move farther afield. Good luck now.'

He looked at the guard, standing at the ready with his green flag. The flag dropped, the engine whistle sounded shrill. The train began to move slowly. We were leaving Ballinasloe for ever.

Even at the age of eight, I was aware that a new chapter in my life was beginning.

1908–9
'Fresh woods and pastures new'

'We're nearly there.' Mother began to fold up the rugs. She took the baskets from the wooden rack. The train journey of forty miles took about two and a half hours from Ballinasloe to Galway. There was a leisurely stop at the intermediate stations. Sometimes a passenger or two got on or off. At Athenry, there was a barefooted woman in a bright red homespun skirt, a black shawl over her head and shoulders. She carried a large deep oval basket of fresh eggs, probably for one of the 'big houses'. There were always mail bags to be loaded and unloaded by the waiting postman. Corridor trains had not come to Ireland, so there were no lavatory facilities on them. A small enamel chamber-pot, discreetly covered by a terry towel, was often carried in a wicker basket. It was used in a case of emergency with children – an emergency never encouraged. Not every station had a 'ladies'. Where there was one, the train made a longer stop, while women and children 'made themselves comfortable', as the euphemism was. The station-master himself usually supervised the passengers getting off the train and saw that everyone was back again before giving the signal to the guard. It was not unusual for the first whistle to signal a false start. As the train began to leave Athenry, hollering and shouting were heard from just outside the station.

'Hold her, hold a minute,' the porter shouted, rushing on to the platform. 'Mr Joyce himself is just a-coming down the road.' On a shout from the station-master, the driver reversed back on to the platform. Mr Joyce, puffing and blowing, came through the barrier.

'Arrah now I've not time for a ticket; I'll get it at Oranmore.'

'Sure that's all right, sor.' A first-class door shut with a bang; there was a whistle and the train started again.

'Here we are at last,' said mother.

The train drew into Galway station. It seemed vast compared with the one in Ballinasloe. It was covered with a domed roof and not open to the sky. At one end was a large sign saying 'Railway Hotel'.

My father was there to meet us with a pony trap and a donkey cart driven by Moran, his new man. The cart was to take the luggage.

Plenty of willing porters loaded up the cart, and we started on the three Irish miles drive to our new home.

'Where's the sea?'

'Oh, it's quite a way. We have to go through the town first.'

'Can we dig by it today?'

Mother laughed. 'Not in this weather. It's much too cold. You can when the summer comes.'

We drove round Eyre Square, the centre of the city: down William Street, past Lynch's Castle, where a former Mayor had, with his own hands, hanged his only son from a window, for treason: into Shop Street, over the bridge and still no sea.

'How soon shall we see the sea?'

'Not long,' encouraged mother, 'we're just getting to Salthill.'

But there was another dreary mile of residential buildings before we came to Salthill. We rounded a bend in the road, and there at last was the sea!

It was so unlike what I had imagined that I could only look at it in amazement. There seemed to be miles and miles of water, slate-grey on this dull December day. Far away in the distance were the mauvish-blue hills of Clare. On our side was the concrete promenade alongside which we were being driven. The tide was coming in. Every few seconds, the long expanse of water advanced a few feet. It was bordered only by white foam as there was no wind. Little peaks of water raced up the beach, some going further than others. Then with a long roar from the turmoiled shingle, the water was pulled back. It left behind some feet of wet sand, shingle and stones, trails of brown seaweed, pieces of flotsam wood and one or two jellyfish, suddenly flabby. However did the sea stay in place without any of the concrete walls which contained the only expanse of water I had ever seen?

Another mile brought us to Gentian Hill House. It was an early nineteenth-century house enclosed by stone walls. It was square built and half covered by Virginia creeper, its red leaves a welcome splash of colour in the greyness of that December day. Iron double gates led into a curved gravel drive in front of the house. A lawn beside the drive was bordered by oak, beech and sycamore trees.

Four tired children were brought into the house. Turf fires had been lit in every room to air the place. Paraffin lamps were already lit, with the wicks turned down, ready to be put up when it got too dark to see.

'Best get the children fed first,' said mother as she began to unpack the large box of groceries that stood on the kitchen table, 'then we can get them off to bed for a bit.'

'Where is the bread?' she asked as she came to the bottom of the box. There was no bread. There had been a mistake somewhere and the nearest shop was two miles away. There was, however, a Jacob's Dundee cake, all covered in almonds and wrapped in silver paper. It was my favourite cake.

'You can have a piece of cake,' said mother, as she began to cut some slices. This should have been a great treat, but fond as I was of sweet stuff, I didn't want cake then: I wanted some bread and butter.

'Reminds us of the story of Marie Antoinette,' said mother.

'A story. Oh, tell us!'

'Well, there was a revolution in France, because people were very poor and had nothing to eat. Marie Antoinette was in her palace. She was the Empress. A large crowd gathered outside shouting. "What are they making that noise about?" asked the Empress.

' "They want bread, ma'am, but there isn't any."

' "Let them eat cake then," said the Empress. There was no cake, of course, for those poor people. But you have some cake. Here you are. We'll get some bread later on.'

We had moved house exactly a week before Christmas. Soon Santa Claus would be coming. He always brought a gauze Christmas stocking filled with sweets and little toys.

'Will Santa Claus know where we are this year?'

'Oh yes. He knows where all children are.'

On Christmas Eve, two large boxes of groceries were delivered and left in the hall. Each was covered with a sheet of brown paper. I was alone. I lifted one sheet of paper and peeped into the box. On top of the groceries were four gauze Christmas stockings!

Disillusionment and a great sadness came on me. In a flash, the mystery of Santa Claus was solved. I was shattered. I dare not tell anyone. I had no business to be prying into the grocery boxes.

Christmas morning came. There was the Christmas stocking on the end of the bed. But Santa Claus had gone for ever.

There came a day fine and mild for December. 'Can we go exploring?'

'Yes, but not outside the back gate,' said mother. We ran out on to the lawn.

'This'll be lovely for playing.' My sister stood in the middle of the lawn, looking round. It was the first time in our lives we had space round the house. For a few minutes we just rushed round and round, jumping, touching one tree trunk, then another. Tired of running, we went through the gate that led into the backyard. On the right was a large grey stone building, stables with a harness-room above.

Moran looked out of the door of the harness-room. He helped my father with the horse, did the garden and odd jobs. 'Do you want to come up?'

'Yes please, yes please!'

'Hold on a while then.'

Moran came down and, one by one, we clambered up the ladder steps into the room. Harness and a couple of saddles hung on the wall. There was a small wooden table and a chair in one corner. Moran began to mix something in a tin.

'What's that you're mixing?'

'Sure it's beeswax and turpentine.'

'Is it for polishing like Mary puts on the floors?'

'The self-same. It's great stuff for keeping the harness right.'

Moran took a saddle and put on some polish. Then with a 'hiss-hiss, hiss-hiss' he rubbed and rubbed with a soft brush until one saw one's face surfaced on the leather.

Mother's voice sounded. 'Where are you, children? Tea's ready.'

Moran put his head out of the loft door. 'They're here, Missus. Come on now,' he said. 'Down with all of you.'

Moran lifted my younger brother and carried him down. One by one the rest of us got down the ladder. It was much more difficult than going up.

'Don't look down,' advised Moran, 'I'm holding on to you.'

It wasn't long before Moran's advice and help became unnecessary. We soon learnt to scuttle up and down that ladder.

One Sunday morning in July, 1910, I woke early. To my amazement, we four children were all in the spare room. I heard someone crying out. It must be mother. I tried the door, but found we were locked in. In response to my rattling of the handle, my father opened the door.

'What's the matter with mother?'

'She's got cramp. She'll be all right in a few minutes. Now, just get back to bed and don't wake the others.' The door was locked again. For a few more minutes I heard the muffled crying-out in the distance and steps on the stairs. Suddenly everything went quiet.

The door opened; my father came in.

'You've got a new sister,' he said.

Though I had seen the birth of kittens and calves from my earliest days, I had not a clue as to where babies came from. I had a naive trust in God's omnipotence and believed He just planted them in the mother's bed. I used to think it would be nice to wake up and find a baby in bed beside me! But somehow, I had made a connection between bed and babies.

One day we were sitting at the tea-table with visitors.

'Has anyone heard what's the matter with Mrs McKay?' someone asked.

'No,' said my mother, 'I just know she's gone to her mother's and is in bed.'

Mr and Mrs McKay lived in the big house across the road from Gentian Hill. They were a middle-aged childless couple.

'I think she may be having a baby,' I volunteered. 'I notice that ladies have babies when they are in bed.'

An icy silence greeted this bit of information. I was guiltily aware that I had not said quite the right thing!

I wrote a letter to my grandma in Ballinasloe, about the new baby. '*Dear Grandma*,' it begins, '*You will be surprised and astonished to hear that we have got a new baby.*'

There follow details of how the doctor brought the baby in a silver box with a spirit lamp underneath to keep her warm. This box was, in fact, the doctor's sterilising bath. The particular use to which I saw it put was just my imagination.

A telegram was sent to my grandparents in Ballinasloe. My sister and I were put on the train in charge of the guard. A kindly lady in the carriage undertook to keep an eye on us. As the train drew out of Galway, this lady suddenly got up and looked out of the window.

'Good gracious,' she said, 'something's on fire. It's Menlough way.'

We looked out of our side window. Billowing clouds of smoke seemed to fill the sky.

It was indeed Menlough Castle on fire. It was the home of the Blakes, a well-known Galway family. The castle was completely destroyed. In the fire Miss Camilla Eliza Blake, the head of the family, perished. My sister Ella was born on a day that was to be long remembered in Galway.

The years that followed until the First World War were indeed the halcyon days of my life, in spite of some ups and downs.

Our house was in a wonderful setting. An inlet of the sea came almost up to the wall of the backyard. One lovely sunny afternoon mother called: 'Put on your sand-shoes. The tide's out. You can play on the shore for a bit. Mind the jellyfish; they can sting.'

Obediently, we put on our sand-shoes to help us down the hundred yards of stony pebbles to the sea. Then the shoes were pulled off and, barefooted, we explored the treasures left behind by the out-going tide. The sea was no more than a foot deep and safe for us to paddle in.

Sometimes jellyfish were stranded. They were of a pinky colour with purple streaks showing through their jelly-like substance. They lay on the sand, flabby, and once out of the water, soon died. Those that had enough water looked like pinky-purple pudding basins swimming about. If they were thwarted, by coming in contact with a human leg for example, one got a very nasty sting. We soon learnt to avoid them.

'Here's Mr O'Connor.' A rumbling sound was heard in the distance. Round the corner came a donkey cart. The cart was small with sides about a foot high, which once had been painted blue. Balanced on the right side of the front was Mr O'Connor, his legs dangling. He was barefooted. His baggy trousers were tied by string about a foot above his ankles. He had on a homespun bawneen, cream, flecked with blue. His tweed cap had the peak at the back of his head. As he stopped, we crowded round.

'What are you getting today, Mr O'Connor?'

'It's seaweed I'm after. It's a grand lot the high tide has thrown up.' He jumped off the cart, took a two-pronged pitchfork from the cart and began to lift long strands of seaweed.

'What's it for?'

'Sure it's great manure for the land.'

'Can we help you?'

'To be sure. Ye can get some of those strands.'

Eagerly, we went to work. We dragged to the cart big heavy strands of seaweed, sometimes three feet long, with a stem two inches thick. Mr O'Connor forked up the lighter stuff. The most ordinary kinds had oval bulges which were fun to burst.

Mr O'Connor soon loaded as much seaweed as the cart could hold, indeed as much as the donkey could pull. Then he showed us some of the seashore treasures.

'Lift up that stone beyont.' He pointed to a biggish stone. We rushed to heave up the stone. It seemed that a myriad of tiny sea creatures dived into a shallow pool, or darted under another stone nearby. Cockles were not able to move so quickly.

'Sure this lot'll be grand for me tay.' Mr O'Connor fetched a tin can hanging from a nail on the cart. He filled it with sea water. Soon he had added to the water about a pound of cockles, their fluted, half-moon-shaped shells closely shut.

'Never take a shellfish if the shell's open,' he warned. 'It means the fish's dead. It's poisonous.'

My favourite seashore treasures were the shells and stones. There were hundreds of tiny shells, cream and pink. There were the empty blue, white-striped shells of razor-fish, true to their name. I still have the scar that resulted from a deep cut made by stepping on one half-hidden in the sand. Occasionally there were large shells, ridged outside but very smooth inside. They were a real find. Put one to the ear and the roar of the Atlantic was clearly heard. Nearly all the stones were oval, worn smooth by centuries of ebbing and flowing tides.

Just then mother appeared, her arms full of towels and bathing costumes.

'Look what I've found!' I held up a smooth stone which had the outline of a small crab on it. Mother looked.

'That's a fossil. Somehow the remains of the crab have got imbedded in the stone. It has probably taken centuries. Now it's time for your bathe. Get into your bathing suits.'

How I dreaded that command! If the weather was reasonable, we had a bathe every day. No matter how warm the water, I came out blue and shivering, hands and feet dead white. Somehow bathing never suited me, but it was considered 'good for you'.

We had only to cross the lane that led to the sea to get on to Gentian Hill, the promontory which gave the name to our house. The hill jutted out into the Atlantic Ocean for about three-quarters of a mile. All along its west side was a grassy walk, bordered by ferns, blackthorn, hawthorn and dense blackberry bushes. Today, it is covered by caravans. Then it was completely unspoilt. Every kind of bird and small wild creature found its home among the bushes. My brothers collected birds' eggs, but it was an unwritten law that only one egg was to be taken from any nest, and then only if three remained. This law was never broken, as far as I know.

We loved the walks on the hill with mother. From her we learnt about the wild flowers.

'Let's see how many different flowers we can find,' she said one day in June. Soon we were all at work and when each had collected a bunch of flowers, we sat down on the stones that lined the path. Mother picked out a tall slender plant with little yellow flowers.

'Who's got this?'

'I have.'

'I have.'

'It's common agrimony, How many petals has it?'

We counted. 'Five.'

'That's right. I see you've got some other yellow flowers. Yes, that one with a leaf in three bits is bird's-foot trefoil. That one Sam has got with only one yellow flower and soft silky leaves is called silverweed. You see the way the leaves look like teeth. They are called serrated.'

Some of the flowers mother did not know, so when we got home we looked them up in an old green book with line drawings. It was called *Flora and Fauna*. That day, between us, we had collected over twenty different wild flowers on the hill.

The only time we met other people on the hill was in March. They were usually Americans who had come to look for the little blue gentians, after which the hill was named. The hill was then covered by these beautiful blue flowers, each about two inches high. They were almost unique in the British Isles.

Mother met a couple one day who had some roots of gentian in their hands. 'I don't think they'll transplant,' said mother. 'I've tried and tried to root some for my sister-in-law. They resist all attempts at being transplanted. It seems they'll only thrive in their native soil.'

'Take care now,' called mother, as we rushed up to the railings that bordered the cliff-end of the hill. Below the cliff, the roar of the Atlantic was heard as its waves broke on the rocks. Opposite the cliff were the hills of Clare. On the right, the three Aran Islands, Inishmore, Inishmaan and Inisheer, were visible on a clear day. Beyond these most western isles, the ocean stretched as far as the eye could see.

Mother turned to us. 'We're exactly opposite America. Strange to think that one day we may be linked by aeroplanes.'

Mother seemed to have an apt quotation for every occasion. This time she quoted from Tennyson:

> For I dipt into the future, far as human eye could see,
> Saw the Vision of the world, and all the wonder that would be.
> Saw the heavens filled with commerce, argosies of portly sail,
> Pilots of the purple twilight, dropping down with costly bale.

Mother paused, and then went on, with the uncanny insight with which she was endowed:

> Heard the heavens fill with shouting, and there rain'd a ghastly dew
> From the nations' airy navies grappling in the central blue.

The tide was on the turn. As sometimes happens at the turn of the tide, the sea was unusually calm and quiet. Even the rocks were untouched by showers of spray. Only gentle lapping of the water's edge was heard. Yet, there is with me still the sense of foreboding that seemed to hang over the calm sea. But the Battle of Britain was still over thirty years in the future.

Ten years later, Alcock and Brown flew the Atlantic. They landed about twenty miles north of the hill on which we were standing. Mother's glimpse into the future was beginning to come true.

1909–12
Galway – 'citie of the tribes'

Change of town meant change of school. My mother had given much thought to our schooling after our move to Galway. She wrote to her sister-in-law on the first day of 1909.

> I am not quite sure what to do about the girls' school. There is the Model School (under the National Board), which is a very good school, a Convent School where the teaching is very good and patronised by some few Protestants . . . Then there is a private school . . . I would like the Model School for a year or two, and the fees are small, but there is the company! By going to the private school, they would be in touch with the Church and children of their own class.

The snob value of the private school won. We went to it for about a year. The building was provided by the Presbyterian Church. It was an early Victorian house in the centre of the town, and on the bank of an inlet of the River Corrib. The only playground was about one hundred square yards of gravel between the front of the house and the stout wall on the river bank. The house was originally the Manse for the Presbyterian minister.

The school, called the High School, catered well for the older pupils who were aiming at a University education. For the younger pupils, it could not have been duller. There were none of the activities nowadays considered essential for children of primary school age. Good handwriting and facility in reading and numeration were the criteria of the education it offered.

My handwriting was very bad. My hand never kept up with my head. I found making careful letters all of the same size, and the crossing of Ts and the dotting of Is very boring.

'I showed this dreadful handwriting to my father,' said Miss Courtney one day. 'He said he was surprised. He thought you could be much better.'

Miss Courtney's father was Dr Courtney, the Presbyterian

minister. He was held in great respect, being a Doctor of Divinity. He was accustomed to pay stately visits to his scattered flock in a hired carriage, a visit always previously arranged. The minister's visit was a highlight in every Presbyterian home. It was Dr Courtney's turn to visit us.

'Dr Courtney's coming this afternoon. I want you to hand round,' said mother one day.

It was just after Miss Courtney's rebuke about my bad handwriting. My heart sank. He'll tell about the writing. He's sure to, I thought.

Dr and Mrs Courtney arrived. The horse was uncoupled by Moran and taken to the stable. In the drawing-room, the best Crown Derby china was set out. There were scones, sponge cake and plum cake, each on one of mother's special hairpin-work doilies. Conversation flowed . . . 'Yes, it has been very mild . . . the crops are well on . . . thank you, I'll have another of these delicious scones . . . how tall the girls are growing!'

Every time there was silence my heart thumped. *He'll begin on the handwriting now.* I passed him sponge cake, plum cake, sponge cake again. Every time I took a plate to him, I expected to hear, *Oh yes, my daughter was telling me about your bad handwriting.* But it never happened. The visit ended happily from my point of view.

Long money sums were my pet aversion. They seemed dull and pointless and a great waste of time.

'Miss Courtney gets the answers out of that book on the desk,' I said to Elizabeth one morning. 'It would save a lot of time if we did.' We were very early in school. I got the book from Miss Courtney's desk.

'Here we are,' I said, 'exercise ten.' We copied the answers neatly. It only took a few minutes, a great saving of time.

Miss Courtney marked my sums. They were all correct. That fact passed without comment. I could get the sums right if I put my mind to them. Then she looked at my sister's book. Her sums were all correct, but she was a year younger, and had not done all the tables, so Miss Courtney became suspicious.

'You copied these from Frances?' she asked.

'Oh, no I didn't. We got the answers from the book.'

'You copied the answers from the book! You copied the answers?' Miss Courtney was incredulous. 'But that's cheating.'

I'd never heard of cheating. I had no intention of doing anything wrong. I simply thought of the answer book as a time-saving device.

I had a bad habit of rolling a pencil up and down the table. It used to annoy Miss Courtney. My punishment for cheating was to roll the pencil up and down the table for half an hour. By the end of the time, I was cured of the habit – even if the moral implications of the word 'cheating' were still not very clear.

The people of Galway were divided by religion into Catholics and Protestants. The Protestants were much in the minority. They, in turn, were divided into three groups, Episcopalians, Presbyterians and Methodists, the last a very small group. We were Presbyterians. The Episcopalian children always seemed to have much more going on. They had a Christmas tree at Christmas: we had nothing.

One year, it was announced that there would be a Christmas party for the children of the Presbyterian Church. We gathered in the largest room of the little High School. The girls in party frocks, mostly of white muslin, sat demurely on one side of the room. The boys, self-conscious in stiff Eton collars, sat on the other side. The Elder of the church entertained us, while the ladies of the congregation got the tea ready. The Elder was a Professor at the University, very learned and very kindly, but entertaining children was not his strongest point. He was small, bald-headed and had a bushy moustache.

He produced a large sheet of paper with an outline of a donkey on it. Each child was given a paper tail with a pin through it and, each in turn, blindfolded, had to try to pin the tail on the donkey's anatomy, as nearly as possible in the right place. Word went round, 'Don't put it anywhere near the donkey.' Even blindfolded, it was easy enough to guess where the donkey was. So all the tails were pinned on the wall remote from the donkey. Somehow the Professor decided the winner, who received a text.

Then came, 'I spy'.

'I spy with my little eye, something beginning with B,' said Stanley when it came to his turn.

'Bell?'

'No.'

'Book?'

'No.'

'Bible?'

'No.'

'Boots?'

'No. D'ye give up?'

'Yes,' we agreed. Inspiration had run out.

'Bald pate,' he said daringly. There was a silence punctuated by a giggle. The Professor pretended not to hear. Fortunately, just at that moment, one of the ladies came in.

'Tea will be ready in five minutes or so.' She made a suggestion. 'Perhaps they would like to sing a hymn while waiting?'

The hard black hymn books with red-bordered leaves were given out. The Professor rummaged through the 'Hymns for Children' section. 'Hymn 575,' he announced.

We found the place and sang:

Here we suffer grief and pain
Here we meet to part again,
In heaven we'll part no more.
Oh, that will be joyful, joyful, joyful
When we meet to part no more.

A sense of the ridiculous, always easily aroused, overwhelmed me. I did not know how to control my mirth, but it passed unnoticed, for the others were really enjoying yelling, 'Oh, that will be joyful'.

Tea made up for the entertainment part of the party. There were none of the savoury things beloved of the modern child. They were not considered good for children. Instead, there were strawberry jam sandwiches, scones, sponge cake, and to end, red and orange jelly with custard.

We had nearly finished, when Mrs de la Poer ffrench (spelt, as she always pointed out, with two little ffs) gushed in, followed by her coachman. He carried a large box.

'I've just come from Dublin. I've brought some cakes for the children from Bewley's.' Bewley's was a well-known confectioners in Grafton Street. 'Sorry I can't stay. I'm dining with Lady Tuam.'

'Goodbye.'

The box was opened. The ladies looked in at the contents. There followed some head-shaking.

'Most unsuitable for children.'

'I suppose we'd better let them have them.'

'They must have cost a fortune.'

So plates of the most luscious cakes were handed round, chocolate-covered, cream-filled.

I took mine, but my eye was bigger than a certain part of my anatomy I must never name. One bite was enough for my small appetite. Then I had a bright idea. I'd put it on my shelf and eat it tomorrow. Next day, the cake had dissolved into a sticky mess.

'Someone must have left it there last night,' I suggested.

'Obviously,' replied Miss Courtney, but did not pursue the matter, much to my relief.

'Go to the cloakroom, and get a bucket and dishcloth.'

It was sad to see a chocolate cream cake ending up in a bucket of water.

There was no dinner break in our school. Children brought with them bread and butter which was eaten about half-past eleven. Then lessons continued until three o'clock. Usually we were fetched by mother or Moran in the pony trap. Sometimes my father needed the trap, so we had to walk the best part of three miles to Gentian Hill. The walk was not without its compensations. It was good to linger on the sea front. There was a mile of beach on the way home. If the tide was out, we looked for large, smooth round pebbles to skim over the water. We competed for the largest number of skims from one stone. The only trouble was that we sometimes got late for our meal and had a scolding for lingering. 'Come straight home' was a daily command.

It was very exciting if, at the spring or autumn equinox, the sea was so rough that it dashed over the promenade and made the road impassable. Then we had to take the long inland way home by Taylor's Hill. On the top of the hill, the raging sea was visible. Breaker followed breaker and broke over the promenade. Seldom was any vessel seen on the grey seething sea. All connected with the sea were good weather forecasters, and knew when it was folly to venture out in boats.

Sometimes my sister and I met Dr O'Shea, the Roman Catholic bishop. He always stopped and had a chat with us, and walked with us if he were going our way.

'What have you been doing in school today?'

'Lamb's *Tales from Shakespeare.* We had the story of Macbeth. Do you know it?' The bishop smiled. 'You ought to read it,' I said, as we walked along. 'It's ever so exciting. You see, Macbeth wanted to be king and it's all about witches and murders and ghosts. And do you know, in the end a wood seemed to be walking towards Macbeth? All the time it was the enemy soldiers holding up boughs of trees and Macbeth got killed.'

We came to the parting of the ways. The bishop was rummaging under his cassock. He took out a little pouch and from it extracted two sixpences.

'Thank you. It does seem an exciting story. Here is something for some sweets.' He offered us the sixpences.

'Oh, no thank you,' I said. 'We're not allowed to take money from strange men.'

'Quite right,' he replied, as he put the money back in the little pouch. 'I expect I'll see your mother one of these days.' He made the sign of the cross over us. The Protestant in me felt uneasy.

He did see my mother, for, to my embarrassment, I heard her tell the story more than once, amidst much laughter. I could not see anything funny in it. But a few days after we met the bishop, two little boxes of sweets arrived for my sister and me.

A diversion once a week was the Band of Hope. This was a teetotal organisation. Its members signed the pledge, that is they promised never to touch strong drink. We all signed quite happily, but without any real understanding of what the pledge meant. The leader usually gave a talk about the evils of drink. Then we had what we really came for, fun and games. Sometimes a member recited a poem or sang a song.

'Who will sing this evening?' asked the leader.

Nobody was willing, so I volunteered. My father had a good tenor voice and we had quite a lot of singing at home. I knew the words of many songs, especially those from *The Students' Songbook.* That particular evening I chose to sing:

Wrap me up in my tarpaulin jacket,
And say, a poor buffer lies low, lies low,
And get you six stalwarts to carry me, carry me,
And drink to this buffer below.

My effort was greeted by a somewhat chilly, 'Thank you.' I, of course, had no idea of the implications of what I had sung. It is only hindsight that tells me it was not the most appropriate song for a meeting of teetotallers!

'Wake up, Frances.' Mother was shaking me. 'Come on, get up. We're going to Dublin to see the King and Queen. Your best clothes are on the chair.' My sister was already nearly dressed.

'I knew yesterday,' she boasted. 'You couldn't be told because you'd be sick.'

I felt a bit of resentment at this. But it was true. If I got excited, I was sick.

We put on our cream serge coats and skirts. The skirt was pleated, the pleats held together on the inside by a wide band of elastic. It was long before the days of permanent pleating. I liked the swing of the pleats as I walked. The jacket had brass buttons.

Our shoes and stockings were brown.

Our breakfast, cocoa and brown bread and butter, was soon over. On went our mushroom-shaped straw hats and cotton gloves. We were ready.

Moran drove us the three miles to the station in the pony trap. The train left at six o'clock, so we started from Gentian Hill at half-past five. The sun was just breaking through the mist that always covered Galway Bay in the early morning. The tide was out. The sand stretched for miles, wet, smooth and grey. On it was one man, barefooted, trousers rolled up above his knees. He had a zinc bucket in his hand. He was collecting cockles or mussels. We saw no one else until we got into the town. The shops were still shuttered. One or two men were hurrying to work, nailed boots making a clatter on the cobbled road. There were more people on the station than usual. They too were going to Dublin, for the royal visit of King George V and Queen Mary. It was 8 July 1911, a few weeks after their Coronation. The Prince of Wales and Princess Mary were coming with their parents. The wooden seats were hard and the train journey seemed endless. The landscape was too familiar; endless fields of ripening corn, in the pasture-land, cows and sheep. The only excitement was an occasional horse galloping away from the noise of the approaching train. Eyes glued to the window, I looked out for the small groups of houses that meant a station was near. Sometimes a woman hanging out washing, or a cowman rounding up a herd, waved at the train. Frantically I waved back. Sometimes a second wave told me that my wave was seen and acknowledged.

There was a long, leisurely stop at each station. They came in turn, musical Irish names: Oranmore, Athenry, Attymon, Ballinasloe, Athlone. At each station, mother looked out to see if there was anyone she knew. All the way we had the carriage to ourselves. I felt disappointed. Someone talking to mother would have relieved the boredom. It was interesting to listen to the conversation of grownups.

'When we get to Mullingar, we'll be more than half-way,' mother encouraged. 'We'll get something to eat there.'

Mullingar came at last. The train stopped for about half an hour. We got out, paid a visit to the ladies' room, and then went into the station restaurant for refreshments. It was a large airy room with tall windows that looked out on the station platform. There were about half a dozen round tables covered with stiffly-starched white damask tablecloths. The two waitresses wore long black dresses and white aprons.

'Good morning, ma'am. Is it going to see the King and Queen ye are?' Mother took the menu card from the waitress.

'Yes. It's a long journey for the girls. I hope the weather keeps up. A pot of tea for me and two glasses of milk for the children. Oh, you've chicken sandwiches. We'll have a plate of chicken sandwiches.'

Mother allowed me a dash of tea in my milk. It helped to get it down. The chicken sandwiches were lovely.

We got to the Broadstone Station about eleven o'clock and took a tram to O'Connell Street. The streets, decorated with red, white and blue bunting and Union Jacks, were already lined with people. We found a good place and waited and waited.

A rumour went round: *They're going to be an hour late.* A visit to Dublin was a rare event. Mother was determined to fit in some shopping.

'I think we'll go to Clery's. I'll get the shopping done before the procession arrives. We'll have to risk getting as good a place.'

We pushed through the crowd. Our good places were taken by others. After waiting for so long, we were sad to lose the places, but it never occurred to us to argue with mother. We went into Clery's, the largest shop in O'Connell Street. It had huge plate-glass windows and balconies on the first floor. We went upstairs to the children's department where we were the only customers.

'What can I show you?' asked the assistant.

'Some everyday frocks to fit these girls. Holland I think.'

'Certainly, madam.' The assistant went off and returned with an armful of frocks. Suddenly, in the distance, came the sound of a band.

'Mother, mother, we're going to miss the procession!' Keen as I was to have a new frock, I was more keen to see the King and Queen.

Mother hesitated. She turned the silver watch she wore pinned on her dress and looked at it.

'Yes, I'm afraid I thought there was more time.'

She looked at the assistant, who stood holding the frocks. 'I think we'll have to leave them . . .'

Just then the frock-coated manager came up to us. 'The procession's coming. If madam would like to take the little girls on to the balcony, I think you would have a good view.'

He opened one of the large casement windows. We joined a few other customers. On an adjoining balcony the shop staff had gathered. It was a grandstand view.

'How lucky we are! I'm glad I decided on the shopping.' Mother drew her chair nearer to the balcony wall. The weather had held, dull but not wet. Down broad O'Connell Street came the procession. It was headed by a pipe and drum band. The saffron plaid kilts of the bandsmen swung in time to the tune. In an open carriage were the King and Queen, with the Prince of Wales and Princess Mary opposite. King George wore a dress suit and grey top hat. Very upright beside him sat Queen Mary. Her cream satin dress fitted her figure tightly. A large jewel on a gold chain glinted on her bosom. Her hat was enormous, broad-brimmed and trimmed with white tulle and ostrich feathers.

I was much more interested in the Prince and Princess than in the King and Queen. The Princess was some years older than I was, but I felt a great affinity with her. Her long brown hair hung loosely over her shoulders far down her back. I wondered if it got tangled, and hurt when it was being combed out after washing. Her hat seemed very like the one I was wearing. I saw myself sitting beside her riding in that open carriage, the crowds cheering and clapping. It must be wonderful to be a princess! Someone gave us Union Jacks. We waved them vigorously over the balcony. The Prince of Wales, charming in his naval uniform, seemed to look up at me. I waved again for him especially.

The procession passed. The crowds began to disperse. We left the balcony and went back to the fitting of holland frocks.

Holland was a hardwearing creamy-brown material. These frocks had inch-high neck bands, trimmed with red and blue Romanian braid. For everyday frocks, they were really quite smart. My frock was extra long to allow for the rate at which I was growing. 'I'll get them off on tonight's post,' said the assistant.

'Thank you, that'll save us carrying them. Please thank the manager for letting us see the procession.'

'Our pleasure, madam. May you have a safe journey back.'

We took the tram back to the Broadstone Station. The train was waiting and already crowded.

As we were looking for a carriage, the station-master came up. 'Well, if it isn't Miss Walker!' He held out his hand. 'Do you remember me? John Watson. You used to teach me.'

For a moment mother looked puzzled. Then she smiled. 'Of course. I recognise you now. But I'm no longer Miss Walker. I'm married and have no less than five children. The girls are the eldest.'

Shyly, we shook hands with him.

'I'll find you seats.' He opened the door of a first-class carriage. What a luxury! Deep-cushioned seats instead of hard boards. We were soon asleep.

I had a vivid dream. The Prince of Wales came to Galway. 'I'm looking for that girl on the balcony who waved to me in Dublin.'

'Come on, wake up. We're home.' Mother was shaking me for the second time that day. Sleepily, we tottered out of the station. Moran was waiting with the trap. The most exciting day of my life was over and I hadn't been sick!

1912–14
More Changes

Mother was driving the three miles into Galway in the pony trap. We caught up with Mrs Woods, who was walking.

'Morning, Mrs Woods. Would you like a lift? We can squeeze you in.' Mrs Woods got into the trap.

'I've been wanting a word with you,' mother went on. 'I'm not at all happy with the way the girls are getting on at the High School. I wish now I'd sent them to the Model School.'

'I know what you mean. It's not really equipped for teaching young children. My five girls have done very well at the Model School. Anyway, we could not have afforded the private school fees for five. I think the school excellent. You couldn't do better than send them there.'

So to the Model School we went. It had been purpose-built for the training of Protestant pupil teachers, who lived in. That is how it got its name. There followed four happy years for me, and an educational foundation for which I am always grateful. I left when I was thirteen.

'Now for homework!' said the English mistress in the next school I attended. 'I want you to write a description of the school you have just left.'

I began my essay with a description of the outside of the Model School.

> The school I went to in Galway is not a very modern one. It is a mixed school and very prettily situated. Anybody seeing it from the road would never think it was a school, but a private building. For the entrance there is just a small iron gate, and a path which is styled 'The Avenue'. Each side of the path there are different kinds of trees which make it very pleasant . . . Some years ago there used to be a bell on top of the school, but that has long been done away with . . .

But another bell there was. It was heavy brass, about eighteen inches high. It had a large mahogany handle with a brass knob on top. There was much competition to ring this bell.

'Can I ring the bell for play, sir?'

'No, you did it yesterday. It's Mary's turn.'

So Mary, or whoever it was, seized the heavy bell and, grasping it with both hands, rang it vigorously, often until Mr Brown shouted, 'That's enough!'

Looking back with the hindsight of an educationalist's experience, I realise that the Headmaster was a gifted teacher, ahead of his time. He had a woman assistant, who taught children up to the age of eight. Then they moved into his class, and could stay there until the age of fourteen.

All, that is about thirty-five of us, were taught in the same large room. It was very high, lit only by four tall windows, all on the south side. Between the two central windows was an enormous clock in a round mahogany frame. The Headmaster had a desk at the far end of the room. It was of oak with a lift-up lid. On it lay the cane, occasionally used. Beside the desk was an enormous blackboard on an easel. That I could neither see the hands of the clock, nor read what was written on the blackboard, I just took for granted. A Mercator's projection map of the world hung on the wall opposite the windows. There was a globe on the mantelpiece. Two tall deal cupboards held such communal books as we had. Pupils bought their own books which were carried to and from school each day in real leather school satchels, always kept well polished. There was no artifical light in the school. My essay describes the heating system:

> . . . In that school, there are no heating pipes,
> just a coal fire, which makes it look very cosy.
> There is a tall guard round the fire.

It was certainly mixed ability teaching. The backgrounds of the parents of the children varied from the artisan to the professional. There was a wide range of ability among the pupils, not of course necessarily dependent on their social status. Considering the limited resources available, the curriculum was surprisingly varied. The boys did woodwork: the girls cookery under the supervision of the infants' mistress. I wrote:

> In winter we have cookery lessons. For that purpose there is
> a nice room fitted up with cupboards, a sink and a gas stove.
> We always eat what we cook, and there is not a girl who
> does not look forward to cookery day.

'Quick march! Halt! St-a-and at ease!'

The commands in broad Irish came from a sergeant-major from the Connaught Rangers. Once a week he took us for drill. The sergeant-major was tall and bulky. He had reddish hair, well plastered down with hair-oil. A reddish moustache matched his hair. The ends of the moustache hung quite three inches long down each side of his mouth. Two medals from the Boer War were fastened on the breast of his khaki tunic. He was a kindly man and we loved his drill sessions. Boys and girls together, we marched, ran at the double, halted, and stood at ease.

This military-type drill was supplemented by gentler sessions with bar-bells and dumb-bells. A bar-bell was a wooden rod about half an inch in diameter and eighteen inches long. There was a knob at each end. 'To the left,' commanded the mistress. The bar-bell was placed upright at the left side. 'To the right,' – the bar-bell went right – 'Up-down-behind.' The commands followed in quick succession.

The dumb-bells, much smaller and heavier, were supposed to develop our muscles. They were used in pairs. Two solid, heavy cubes of wood were joined by a thick piece of dowel, just thin enough to be grasped. They were clashed above the head, behind the back, to the right, to the left, at the mistress's command.

Music, if such it could be called, accompanied these exercises. It came from a wheezy harmonium, the only musical instrument in the school. The mistress combined playing the harmonium with calling out the drill commands. It is one of my regrets that we never received any musical training. Certainly we did some singing. A large sol-fa chart was hung up. I could just see it. 'Soh-me-lah-soh-soh: soh-me-lah-soh-doh' is the one tune I remember. No one explained the relationship between the symbols and I always felt we were singing gibberish.

Mr Brown's general knowledge was vast. He taught all the academic subjects. He encouraged wide reading and gave us the elements of science. 'You've all got very wet this morning,' he told us one day. 'How much rain fell since yesterday? Anyone know?'

No one did. 'We're going to make an instrument today that will tell us.'

So, with a glass cylinder and an empty tin can, we made a crude rain gauge. Every day we recorded on a chart the amount of rain that had fallen. It was very seldom the rain gauge was completely empty.

Another day he came in with a pile of home-made manuscript books. Each was covered in bright wallpaper. 'These are your "best" books. When you have written a good composition, you can copy it into your best book.'

What a simple incentive! Into those books went compositions, stories, current affairs, nature notes and the occasional poem. They were proudly shown to the inspector.

The visit of an inspector made a nice change. He came once a year. We liked inspectors with a good sense of humour. That was a virtue Mr O'Neill lacked. In 1913, ball-point pens had not been invented: fountain pens were forbidden, even if a pupil was the proud possessor of one. Pen nibs were therefore of great importance. There was one well-known maker of steel pen nibs – every magazine and newspaper carried a rhyming advertisement for them.

Mr O'Neill was testing our general knowledge. It was my sister's turn for a question. 'What comes as a boon and a blessing to men?' he asked.

'Women,' said my sister promptly. With the headmaster's eye on us, no one dared to giggle.

'Oh, go to Hong Kong or wherever you live,' was his astonishing remark on receiving this bit of information. 'Next.'

James Tennant knew the answer: 'The Pickwick, the Owl and the Waverley pen.'

There were no public libraries in Galway. Reading was the chief source of entertainment, certainly among the Protestant community. Most houses possessed a fair supply of the standard classics: Dickens, Scott, Jane Austen, Mrs Gaskell. A green book called *The Royal Reader Standard VI* introduced us to a miscellaneous collection of literature and general knowledge. There were extracts from Shakespeare, *Religio Medici*, Wordsworth, Browning and other Victorian poets. At the back of the book were several columns of Greek and Latin roots.

'You're supposed to have learnt five Greek roots this week. We'll see who has,' Mr Brown said every Friday. 'James, give out the slips.'

James handed round long narrow pieces of paper. 'Ready? Write down the meaning of "anthropos".'

Those who had done their homework wrote. Those who had not, hoped for a bit of help from a neighbour.

'Well, Louisa?'

'A man, sir.'

'Good! Now write down an English word derived from "anthropos". Pens down!'

'Hands up. You, Alex.'

'Anthropology.'

'Yes, that's it. How many got it right?'

'H'm . . . some haven't done their homework. We'll see what a few minutes at playtime will do. Who'd like the dictionary to find some more words from anthropos?'

There was only one dictionary in the school. It was large and heavy, its cover protected by one of black cloth. Dictionary work was popular. Under the guise of consulting about the meaning of a word, it was possible to do quite a bit of gossiping, especially if one could manoeuvre to pair off with one's best friend. The results of the research were put on the blackboard.

How often I have been grateful, when faced with an apparently unknown word, for that list of Greek and Latin roots, so easily learnt in childhood!

The reading book included, among other Shakesperian pieces, a long extract from *Julius Caesar*. It was Mark Antony's speech at Caesar's funeral.

'Some of you like to act it?' asked Mr Brown, after we had read and discussed the scene. Those of us who wished to act were left to our own devices. Mr Brown could not leave the rest of the class.

I loved acting – though my mother's Puritan upbringing made her uneasy about it. The acting was voluntary. It was difficult to get the boys to take part and few wanted the bother of learning so much just for fun. In those days learning by heart came easily to me. So did organising. Whenever I hear or read that speech of Mark Antony's, I recall the day we acted it. I took the part of Mark Antony, and was producer, prompter and dresser as well.

Boys could be persuaded to be citizens, the only other characters in the scene, and there was no lack of volunteers for Caesar's body. There it was, more or less inert, on the floor. It was wrapped in a toga made of an old sheet liberally bedaubed with red ink.

'See what a rent the envious Casca made,' I declaimed holding up one end of the red-ink stained sheet and pointing to a big tear in it. 'Through this the well-beloved Brutus stabbed!' Another bit of the sheet was held up showing a much larger hole. The irony of *Brutus is an honourable man* was not lost on me.

'Look you here –' pointing to the body – 'keep still. Here is himself, marred as you see with traitors.'

At a whispered prompt, the citizens joined in:

'O piteous spectacle!'

'O noble Caesar!'

'O most bloody sight!'

'We will be revenged: – revenge, – about, – seek, – burn, – fire, – kill, – slay, – let not a traitor live!'

So keen were the citizens on revenge that the scene got out of hand. Mr Brown looked in.

'Time for Mental Arithmetic.'

How real it all was! What an introduction to Shakespeare! That children should be allowed to act is taken for granted in a modern school. I suggest that it was almost unique in a National Board School in 1913.

'I'll hate leaving here, but I suppose it's inevitable,' I overheard my mother say to my father.

'I think when you get there, you'll find the advantages.'

'Perhaps.' My mother did not sound convinced. As I was not supposed to hear this conversation, I dare not ask where we were going.

Much as we all loved Gentian Hill House, it had one big disadvantage – its distance from the town. There was no telephone, so anyone requiring my father's services had either to send a telegram, or come in person. The yard was not really adequate for my father's practice. There were no stables where sick animals could be housed.

About a fortnight later, mother came into our playroom. She put down an orange box divided into two by a thin wooden partition.

'Now, you two girls, get all your books and possessions together. The remover is coming first thing tomorrow morning. You can have half the box each.'

Next morning, we left in the pony trap for our new home. It was about a mile the other side of the town. We passed the station, the Roman Catholic chapel, the Magdalen Asylum which ran a laundry, worked by 'fallen girls', then up a hill. As we turned the corner at the top of the hill, mother pointed to a tall house in the distance. It stood by itself on a gentle hill. 'There's Wellpark,' she said.

Wellpark was a rambling Victorian house, standing in about twelve acres of poor rocky land. It overlooked Lough Atalia, an inlet of Galway Bay. The house got its name from a fresh-water well in the middle of one of the fields. There was no main water supply: we depended on the well for fresh water. A pump in the yard was hand-operated every day for an hour, to keep the house supplied with drinking water. To this day, when I turn a tap on, I am often conscious of the need not to waste water.

The house had three storeys of large rooms connected by long corridors. 'I wish whoever built the house had thought of the needs of a large family,' my mother often said.

For in spite of its size, the house had only four bedrooms, and one of those was quite poky. But the house was full of new excitements for us children, and particularly under the stairs. Here there was a large room and passages from it which went under most of the house. We played games of 'murder' and developed photographs with hypo. They were taken with my small five-shilling Brownie camera. I never had a better camera, but alas, one of my brothers dropped it in a stream while he was trying to photograph a fish. It was never the same again.

The big yard was surrounded by outhouses, stables, haylofts, grain stores. Over two of the stables was a large hayloft with two trap-doors. It was usually full of hay for the cows. We were forbidden to play in this loft, because part of the roof was unsound. However, we often disobeyed, as we loved to roll about in the hay, another forbidden activity.

One Easter Saturday, mother had gone to town shopping, my father was out, I was reading. Suddenly my elder brother rushed in.

'Come quickly, Alec has fallen through the trap-door in the hayloft.'

My sister and I ran out. There was Alec sitting on the stable floor, looking very dazed. He had just missed a mangold-cutting machine by inches. While we were wondering what to do, mother appeared as if by magic. She said little until it was clear that Alec was only suffering from shock.

'Now, let it be quite clear to you all,' she said, 'the hayloft is out of bounds, as indeed you very well know.' In spite of the warning, Alec fell out of the loft a second time, and for the second time escaped with a few scratches.

Once a year, on the occasion of the annual Galway Races, we *were* allowed to go into the hayloft. This was a great social event, which brought people from all over Ireland and, indeed, from farther afield. The racecourse was about a mile up the road from our house. All the traffic had to pass by Wellpark. In the hayloft was a door which opened on to the road below. We were allowed to have this door open and see all that passed. Sidecar after sidecar came by, overloaded with as many as six people aboard. The horses strained as they pulled their heavy load up the slight hill. Donkey carts went at a slower pace. In and out of the horse traffic went the motor cars of the well-to-do, usually Fords. Occasionally a Rolls-Royce, with its gleaming brass lamps and figure poised on the bonnet, came by. It was always driven by a uniformed chauffeur. The Rolls would be greeted with a cheer as the traffic halted to let it pass. Pedestrians streamed along, keeping close to the walls as there were no footpaths.

Nearly everyone gave us a wave.

My brothers loved to play a trick on the pedestrians. A purse was lowered on a thread to the road below. Then just as someone attempted to pick it up, it disappeared, pulled up by the thread.

My father always went to the races in an official capacity. If a horse met with an accident which meant it had to be destroyed, it was my father's job to shoot it. I cannot remember this ever happening, or if it did, I was not told. My mother also went to the races, but she had scruples about betting. After one racing day, she came back with thirty shillings.

'Here you are,' she said, 'here's half-a-crown each. You are to spend it at the Red Cross Fête. I can't keep money won by gambling.' She had picked the winner of a race, a complete outsider, who came in at sixty to one.

'What ever made you bet on that horse?' she was asked.

'Oh, I liked the silver and blue of the jockey, so just for fun I put sixpence on him, never dreaming he'd win!' We thoroughly enjoyed ourselves at the fête.

With larger premises, my father was able to treat many more animals on the spot. There was nearly always a pet cat in residence.

One lady brought along her very fat grey cat. 'He won't even look at a bit of chicken,' she complained. Chicken was a great luxury in those days.

'Leave him to me,' said my father. 'He'll be right as rain by next week. Most of the cats I'm asked to treat have nothing the matter but overfeeding.' For two days the cat had nothing but milk and water. Time after time a week of almost starvation diet meant complete recovery for the animals. It was of course, only the well-to-do who could afford the vet.

One of the fascinating things to be seen in the yard was the slinging of a horse. It was before the days of general anaesthetics, though I believe my father sometimes used chloroform. If he wanted, for instance, to castrate a horse it had to be inverted. There was a contraption which consisted of a long cross beam, supported at each end by two others. In the middle of the cross beam was a pulley. A broad canvas band, called a cradle, was put round the horse's body. Each end of the cradle had a large eye. Through these was put a hook suspended from the pulley. Then the rope of the pulley was gently pulled, and suddenly the horse was upside down, suspended in the canvas sling. Its legs, which had been loosely fettered, were sticking up in the air. We were never allowed to see whatever it was my father did.

We were never bored. There were plenty of things to do and places to explore. My two brothers and a friend came bursting into the sitting-room one day. Mother was sewing.

'Look, mother, see what we've found.' They held up two skulls.

'Where on earth did you get those?'

'In the woods up by Joyce's Lodge. There's a sort of graveyard. There's lots and lots of skulls about.'

Mother stopped her sewing. 'It's desecration. Take them straight back to where you found them.'

So, dejectedly, the three boys went off to return the skulls. What eventually happened to all those skulls? The old graveyard is now the site of a large council estate.

In the distance sounded the whirl of bagpipes. 'Come on,' we called to each other, 'there's a military funeral.'

On the hill opposite Wellpark was the cemetery. It had a Protestant portion and a Roman Catholic portion, and we could see the Protestant portion from the top bedroom window. We often watched a funeral through binoculars. The military funerals were particularly spectacular. A detachment of the Highland Light Infantry was stationed in the Renmore barracks near us. There were several funerals, often the result of the violence. First came the band playing the 'Dead March' from *Saul*, the heavy tread of the accompanying soldiers keeping time with the march. The gun carriage followed. On it was the coffin covered by a Union Jack. Six bearers, three each side, had reversed rifles. After the interment, which we could not see, came the sounding of the 'Last Post', the notes lingering over the hill. Finally the pipers played 'The flowers of the forest are a' wede awae'.' Though we looked on the funeral as entertainment, we always left the window in quietness. Young as we were, we could not fail to sense something of the mystery of mortality.

Mother came into the schoolroom where I was curled up on the old sofa reading. She had an opened letter in her hand. 'We're going to England to stay with your uncle and aunt.'

'Who's going?'

'Just you and I for a week. You *might* go to live with them and go to school there.'

The implication of the 'might' was not explained to me. I was a child who got easily excited and then got sick. So I was never told beforehand of any event that was exciting. Going to England was exciting.

'Go and pack your personal things in your little case. Your clothes can go in with mine in the big case.' Mother put the letter back into the envelope.

I rushed upstairs to pack my little case. It was a Christmas present, but I had not been able to use it. It did not take long to put my brush and comb and washing things in the case. I was not able to get the case to shut. Mother came in. I asked her for help.

'It's too full. What ever have you got in it?'

'Books for the journey.'

'You can't possibly take all those books with you. One's enough.' Reluctantly, I took out my favourite books. Which one should I take? *Stepping Heavenward* was very heavy. Mother didn't think much of Angela Brazil. In the end I decided on *Little Women* – I always identified with Jo. With the pile of books out of it the case shut easily.

One book was enough. Much of the long journey was by night. In spite of a choppy Irish Sea, and a boat without stabilisers, I slept most of the way.

We arrived at my aunt's house. She was one of the first school doctors and had been appointed to Birmingham. Her 'Chief', as she called him, was Dr Auden, whose son Wystan became a poet. Two days later, I was taken to a big school and left at the door. A red-haired maid in a black dress and white starched apron showed me where to hang my coat. Then, following a crowd of girls, I found myself in a big hall, the like of which I had never seen. In it were rows and rows of desks. It had a platform at one end. On the wall behind the platform was a large plaque. It showed a lion and a unicorn facing each other. Between them were two shields with a crown on top of them. The lion also wore a crown. At the bottom of the plaque were the words *Dieu et mon droit*, and on a scroll connecting the lion and the unicorn there was the statement *Honi soit qui mal y pense*. I had not learnt any French, and the only word which made any sense was *Dieu*.

'They'll ask you to do some sums and a composition,' was all my mother had told me when she left me at the door. A mistress gave out some sheets of blank paper and a printed sheet of arithmetic questions. 'Begin at number one and do as many sums as you can,' she said.

I had started on my first examination. Strange to say, I had never come across an examination before. We did not have them in the Model School. Instead, we took home every week a 'Judgement Card'. This contained all the marks we had gained during the week. It had to be brought back on Monday signed by a parent or guardian. It was not unknown for a pupil who got bad marks to forge a signature, but the deception seldom got past Mr Brown.

No one told me that I was, in fact, competing for a place in a King Edward VI Grammar School. As it was, I was in my element, and not in the least worried. I gave the examiners information on gun-running in Ireland, told them how to spring-clean a room, wrote on my favourite book and completed lines of poetry. One line I remember was: *Hope springs eternal in the human breast*. Thanks to my mother's love of verse, I could add, *Man never is, but always to be blest.*

Back I went to Galway and the Model School. About a fortnight later, there was a loud knock on the schoolroom door. 'See who's there,' said Mr Brown, looking from the blackboard and nodding to the boy nearest the door. Robert opened the door.

'A telegram for you, sir,' he said, holding up the orange envelope.

A hush fell on the class. No one liked telegrams. They usually brought bad news. We all watched while Mr Brown tore open the orange envelope and read the message on the white paper.

His face lighted up. 'There's no answer,' he called to the telegraph boy waiting at the open door. Mr Brown waved the telegram. 'What do you think it says?'

No one knew of course.

'Well, it's to say that Frances has got a place in a school in England. That's an honour for us. Who'd like some extra playtime to celebrate?' All hands shot up.

'All right, you can go for an extra quarter of an hour.'

Don't imagine there was a mad rush for the door. No one dreamt of such a thing! Exercise books were closed and passed to the end of the row to be collected by the pupil in the last desk. History books were passed to the other end. The brass lids on the inkwells went down with a clatter. Pens and pencils were put into wooden pencil boxes. As each desk was cleared and tidy, the occupant sat with folded arms. Impatient looks were given to the slow-coaches.

When there was dead silence, 'Stand!' said the master. 'Turn.' All turned to the right. 'Lead on,' he said to the boy nearest to the door. In an orderly silence, row after row filed out into the playground.

What a change for me outside!

I was usually a gift for teasing by the boys. It was common for me to be called 'Four-eyes', or 'Lamp-post'. That day it was 'Good old Frances'. I was somewhat bewildered as to what all the fuss was about.

All the other children knew or cared about was that I had won some extra playtime. But, in a sense, it was my glorious hour and I enjoyed it!

1914–15
An English interlude

On 14 September 1914, I went up the steps of that school in England for the second time. The same maid was at the door. She checked my new sailor hat, my white blouse, my gym slip nearly down to my ankles to allow for the rate at which I was growing.

'Where are your gloves?' she asked.

'I haven't any, it's not cold.'

'You have to wear gloves. Don't come tomorrow without them or you'll get an order mark.' I'd no idea what an order mark was, but was soon to find out.

In Ireland, we only wore gloves to church or if it was cold. She let me in, and I found my peg under the Ms. Then a mistress lined us all up.

'Where are we going?' I asked the girl in front.

'Take an order mark,' said the mistress.

'What did she say?' I asked.

'Take another order mark,' barked the mistress.

'What's an order mark?' I persisted.

'Ssh,' said the girl, but her warning was too late.

'Take another order mark and go to the Headmistress.'

Mystified, I got out of the line and somehow found my way to the Headmistress's office.

'Well?' she said.

'I was told to come to see you.'

'What for?'

'I got three order marks.'

'Three order marks! What were you doing?'

'I don't know. I was only asking where we were going.'

'Oh, you're that Irish girl. Do you know what an order mark is?'

'No. I've never heard of them.'

She was quite kindly and explained to me that there must be silence in the corridors. I was very used to silence in classroom at home, but no one ever bothered about the corridor.

'An order mark is given if you talk. Three order marks make a conduct mark. If you get a conduct mark, you must report to me.' She did not cancel the conduct mark, which appeared on my first report.

It took me some time to adjust to this new school, so different from the happy, friendly place I had left. The discipline was regimental. The teaching methods were up-to-date but new to me, especially in arithmetic. I was ahead of the class in arithmetic, but found that answers attained by my methods were not acceptable. The correct answer was not what mattered but how it was obtained. I had to transform my copybook hand-writing into script and learn to write on double lines. Accustomed to writing several pages of composition, I found this script very frustrating, and got into much trouble for writing on top of the double lines. I had done no French and was plunged into a second-year class. The only new subject I started at scratch was Latin. I loved it, though was sorry that I could not do cookery as well.

The school, however, had its compensations. There were lots of new activities in which to take part. I threw myself wholeheartedly into everything that was going on.

'You need not worry about Frances,' my uncle wrote to my mother, 'she seizes life with both hands.'

I particularly enjoyed tennis and swimming.

'Can you swim?' asked the PE mistress.

'No,' I said, 'but I can float.'

'I'm surprised,' she replied. 'And you a girl from the Atlantic coast.' I don't think she had any idea of what the sea on the Atlantic coast was like.

I was put into the beginners' class. The swimming bath was a revelation to me with its warm water bounded by solid walls. It was most unlike the sea at Galway, with its sudden treacherous depths and, more often than not, angry rolling waves. I got into the swimming pool and, to my surprise and that of the mistress, swam the width straight away.

I lived with my aunt and uncle, a brother and sister. My aunt, against all odds, had qualified as a doctor. They were both liberal in politics and religion. She had a strong social sense and I began to catch it. I became acutely aware of the plight of the under-privileged.

We went to a fair in aid of the Red Cross. There were roundabouts, coconut shies, and hoop-la. I was given half-a-crown to spend on these. On the way, I came across a stall of baskets made by the blind. As I looked at the stall manned by blind people, I remembered my aunt coming to visit us in Galway, some years before. She was very interested in eyes.

'You're all having your eyes tested,' mother said one day. So, in the dining-room, my aunt set up her eye-testing apparatus.

'Just as I expected,' she said at the end, 'Frances is very short-sighted.' Soon after, mother and I had a trip to Dublin, to see an oculist in Merrion Square, the equivalent of London's Harley Street. The night before, I had drops put in my eyes. The resulting blurriness of sight spoilt the excitement of the trip.

About a week later a pair of steel-rimmed glasses arrived. I put them on. I was filled with wonder at what I could see. The gravel on the drive was no longer a vague dark mass. I could see tiny individual stones, light grey, slate-blue, with here and there larger pebbles of mottled cream. I could see the shape of the leaves on the oak tree. The birds were no longer blurs, but feathered creatures with wings, yellow feet and beady eyes.

Blind people became very real to me. So at that fair, I spent the whole half-crown on one of their baskets.

'Oh dear!' said my aunt, 'I think you're too young for this sort of thing.' But the basket gave me great satisfaction.

I'd always been fond of acting and getting up little entertainments. So I collected the children round about and got up an entertainment in aid of the Red Cross. It was in my aunt's house. It produced thirty shillings. The Headmistress heard of it and sent for me. 'I'm so glad to see girls taking an interest in social affairs.'

She was a diminutive Scot, and always dressed in brown, her skimpy iron-grey hair dragged into a hollow bun ring on the top of her head. I had not thought of what was great fun as a social activity. Indeed, I didn't know what she meant. But I thought she was very nice, and not a bit like the ogre she was generally considered by my contemporaries.

It had always been impressed on me that I was neither musical nor artistic. I loved singing, but was always afraid to sing.

'You're flat,' said the teacher at the Model School one day. From that day until I was quite middle-aged I was afraid to sing in public, in case I was flat. Looking back, I must have been all right at the Grammar School for, at the end of my first year, I was one of those transferred to the singing class of the Senior Music master.

Art at the Model School was another of my dreads. I never

could get a sphere balanced on top of a cube to look like either. When the whole form at the Grammar School was put in for some national art examination, I felt I didn't care. I was sure to be bottom.

'Draw a boy kicking a football,' we were asked.

That was new. I had never tried such a subject, though I had seen lots of boys kicking footballs. Not caring, I just drew a few lines. Imagine my amazement when I got 'Distinction'. It seemed a fluke, and probably was.

Such experiences in my own education gave me a particular insight when I became a teacher. How wrong it is to label a child this or that, before its potential has been given an opportunity of fulfilment at its own level. It was not until I was in my seventies that a modicum of both musical and artistic ability was encouraged by sympathetic teachers in evening classes.

The war was in its first few months. It seemed to have little effect on life in general. Food had not yet become scarce. Occasionally, bands of soldiers passed by, singing 'Good-bye Dolly, I must leave you'. There was optimism everywhere: *It will all be over by Christmas*.

'Would you like to hear Clara Butt sing?' asked my uncle.

'Who's she?'

My uncle was horrified. 'You don't know who Clara Butt is! She's the greatest singer in the world. We'll go to hear her on Sunday.'

Clara Butt was giving an open-air concert in the centre of Birmingham. A grand piano stood on a raised dais. An area surrounding the dais had been roped off. In company with some other children, I was pushed to the front line of the crowded audience. I had a very good view, but was conscious of the rope cutting into my waist. I was quite the tallest child among those standing by me.

A great wave of clapping greeted the appearance of the singer, who was large and tall, and dressed in a long black gown. She sang 'Land of Hope and Glory' in a deep contralto voice, and with great conviction. It was the first time I had heard it. I thought it most inspiring. The song closes with the lines:

God who made thee mighty,
Make thee mightier yet.

As the deep notes soared above the crowd and faded, a great wave of emotion and patriotism was let loose. Clapping and calling, the crowd surged forward. Under the pressure from

Above: My maternal grandparents, Sarah and Alexander Dods, about 1912.
Below: My mother in 1915.

Above: My father in his R A V C uniform in 1918.

Below: 'The house where I was born', Dunlo Street, Ballinasloe in 1977. The ground floor is now an electrician's shop.

Above: With Elizabeth (left, holding a doll), in Ballinasloe about 1905.

Below: Gentian Hill house, Salthill, Galway, to which we moved in 1908. It is now a guest house.

Above left: The Moffett children about 1911. Left to right, Ella, Elizabeth, myself, Sam, Alec.

Below left: The white house dwarfed by the warehouses was the Girls' High School, Galway.

Above: The Claddagh, Galway, before the First World War.

Below: Wellpark, our second Galway home.

Left: The photograph opposite was taken on my last day in England in 1915. The picture of my mother on the first page was taken at the same time.

Above: University College, Galway.

Below: The Moffett children in 1919, shortly after the death of mother. I am seated in the chair.

In 1922 everyone in my class who graduated had a photo like this to celebrate the occasion.

behind, the rope began to cut more deeply into my thin body. I remembered no more until I found myself lying on the ground inside the roped-off enclosure. My uncle and a policeman were standing over me. Clara Butt, on her way down the steps, turned and looked at me and said something. What it was I did not hear.

It was very near the end of the summer term, 1915. My mother had come over from Ireland to take me home for the holidays.

Once again, I was sent for by the Headmistress. I now knew her quite well. I had sent her a Christmas card with a quotation on it from Ben Jonson. It was one of my aunt's castoffs. She was quite horrified when she heard I had sent it to the Headmistress. It said: *True happiness consists not in the multitude of friends, but in the worth and choice.* 'I'm glad you count me among your friends,' she said when she thanked me for the card. 'I've just had a long talk with your mother. She wants you to leave and go back to Ireland,' were her words on this occasion.

I was taken aback. I did know that my mother was not happy about my separation from the rest of the family. It was becoming increasingly dangerous to cross the Irish Sea because of the German submarines. It looked as if I could not go home for the holidays.

'Aren't you happy here?'

'Yes, I like it.'

'Well, do you want to leave?'

I was torn by conflicting emotions. The child in me wanted to go back to the family. But I had adjusted well and had settled down. I thoroughly enjoyed the many activities I knew I would not have in Ireland.

'I don't know,' I murmured, and it was the truth.

'Well, if you go, your chance of Girton is gone.'

I went and it was.

Growing up

I am fourteen.

The autumn of 1915 saw me making a second adjustment in a year to new school ways.

'You're rather behind in French and mathematics,' said the Headmistress of the little Protestant High School to which I was now going. 'You'll have to work hard to catch up.'

It was true. I found that I was really behind my contemporaries, except in Latin. But I had gained a width of experience in my English interlude. I had seen for myself the Crown Jewels in the Tower of London. I had whispered in the gallery in St Paul's Cathedral. I had learnt, by actually seeing it, Wren's epitaph round the dome: '*si monumentum requiris, circumspice*'. I had heard wonderful music for the first time, in candlelit King's College Chapel, Cambridge. The walks along the Cherwell in Oxford were to give reality to 'The Scholar Gypsy' we studied in the following year. So I settled down happily enough to prepare for the first of a series of examinations – one every year for the next seven years.

At home there was no censorship of books or newspapers, but in spite of all I read I was extraordinarily ignorant of the facts of life. The learning process began when I was about twelve, and on a visit to my maternal grandparents.

I was out for a walk with Olive Brown, a girl about a year older than I was. We had just met Mrs Conway who was wheeling out her baby girl. As Mrs Conway went on, Olive suddenly said to me: 'Do you know where babies come from?'

'Well, I think so,' I replied, for I had my own answer to that question.

'I've found out for sure,' went on Olive. 'When you are about thirteen something will happen to you. Then if a man puts his arms round your waist, you'll have a baby. Swear you'll not tell anyone I've told you.'

I swore. Olive did not give me any more information: probably she had no more to give. She had shattered another illusion and left me feeling guilty, confused and, for several years, absolutely scared if a man even touched me.

I had imagined that a baby dropped from the skies into its mother's bed.

Where have you come from, baby dear,
Out of the nowhere into here

said the nursery rhyme. I took it literally.

Because we were the children of a veterinary surgeon, and saw animal mating and birth frequently, I think my mother assumed that we would make the logical connection between animal and human procreation – but I, at least, never did. This, apart from the reticence of my mother's generation, was partly due to the fear given me by Olive.

It was reinforced by something said to me by my mother: 'I'd rather go to your funeral than your wedding.'

I was too young to know, and never did know, what unhappiness prompted such a remark.

So I was scared of growing up. Many years later, I was helping my doctor aunt clear out her attic, and came across a couple of bundles of a pamphlet she had written in 1890. The print was close and small. '*What we should tell our girls*' was the title, black on the purple cover. A quick glance through the pamphlet showed me how good and clear it was.

'Aunt,' I said, 'having written this, how could you let me live with you for a year when I was fourteen in such ignorance?'

'Were you ignorant?' she replied. 'I never knew. I did my best more than once to try to find out. Each time you said, "I know all I want to know, thank you". I even left this pamphlet in your room. I'd hoped you'd read it.' I hadn't. It was so unattractively presented that I suppose I ignored it. There were plenty of more interesting-looking books about.

A good deal of whispered conversation went on among the girls in school. I was never involved in it. For one thing, I liked looking after the small children in the short playtime we had. 'Oh, go away. You're too innocent,' I heard more than once. Innocent of what, I wondered.

One day, when I was about fifteen, I came across a pile of books on the sideboard in the dining-room. A piece of brown paper and some string lay on top of them, evidently to pack up the books. Always curious about books, I opened the first one. It only took a few minutes' quick reading and a look at the diagrams for the light to dawn. The whole process of procreation became quite clear and quite logical, considering what I'd always known about domestic animals. However, I felt guilty about the knowledge I'd gained. For one thing, I'd no business to be prying into parcels. By evening, the books had disappeared. Mother had not considered them suitable, I suppose.

The burden of being the eldest weighed heavily on me. 'You're the eldest, you should know better,' I heard many times. Yet I knew being the eldest brought privileges. These I often thought were unfair. The eldest must choose. I was very young when I first felt this was very unfair on my sister. Indeed, I believe that later we always took turns in choosing.

I do not know how far I was an odd child at school. I was somewhat self-conscious of my height and thinness. At fourteen, I was five foot eight inches tall and weighed only seven stone. I was aware that I was plain, and a pair of steel-rimmed glasses half-way down my nose did not enhance my looks.

'Who's the prettiest girl in the school?' was a favourite game. My sister always won. 'Who's the plainest?' I always won, but felt no resentment.

My sister, a year younger, was much the stronger personality. She should have been the eldest. She had a keen moral sense and never seemed to do anything wrong. I often had a craving for sweet stuff. We got little, as it was considered bad for us. One day, I stole a sweet biscuit. My sister caught me.

'I'm not going to tell,' she said, 'but you must bury it.' She took me into the garden where I buried the forbidden biscuit.

I was having a struggle to catch up in French after my year in England. One evening, my sister and I were consulting about some French exercise.

'I think it's *il faut partir*,' I said.

'No it's not,' replied my sister confidently. I crossed out what I had written and put in what she suggested.

Next day, the teacher was going over the exercise with me. 'Why did you cross that phrase out?' she asked. 'It was quite right.'

'My sister said it was wrong.'

'When are you going to stop depending on your sister? She has beauty, but you have brains; use them!'

I didn't believe I had brains, but that comment marked a turning point. I began to rely much more on my own judgement.

Boys did not come into the picture until we were well on in the teens. As my sister's good looks developed, they were round her like bees round a honey-pot. On the way into town was the Boys' Grammar School. It had a large number of boarders from all over the West of Ireland. Suddenly, my sister and I developed a keen interest in evening church. For the school boarders it was compulsory. They marched in a crocodile to the church, about three-quarters of a mile away. Each boy wore a black suit, an Eton collar and a bowler hat.

Coming back, the crocodile went ahead of us, and disappeared through the large wooden gates. However, the playing field extended towards our house for several hundred yards. About two hundred yards along, two or three boys leapt over the wall and accompanied us most of the way home. My sister was, of course, the attraction. She had at least two companions. I remember trailing behind with a rather shy boy, no doubt pressed into service.

One Sunday evening we met my father. This was unexpected, as he liked to spend Sunday evening at home unless he were out on a case. He raised his hat and went on, without stopping.

Rather fearfully we waited, but nothing was said that night. Next day, my mother said: 'I don't like these meetings you're having with boys. They'll get into trouble for being out of bounds. I've seen the Headmaster. He has agreed that boys may come to tea on a Sunday.' My mother was, in this as in other things, ahead of her time.

So, for many Sundays to come, there were always boys for Sunday tea, ostensibly my brothers' friends. I never had a boy-friend. I couldn't imagine anyone wanting me.

Adolescence brought with it many fears. As family after family lost someone in the war, I became acutely aware of its horrors. My greatest fear was that I might be eighteen before it was over. Then I should have to go as a nurse, or so I thought. This I dreaded because of a phobia about blood. We were all at dinner one day. My father was carving a joint of beef.

'Did you hear what happened?' mother asked. A young girl, the only child of some people my parents knew, had been killed in a riding accident.

'Nobody knows why the pony bolted,' said my father. 'The girl fell off, but her foot caught in the stirrup. She was dragged along the ground. She died of a lacerated brain.'

'Only thirteen.' Mother glanced at us. 'I do feel for the poor parents.'

'What's a lacerated brain?' asked my sister.

As my father explained, everything began to fade away. I crashed across the dining-table, knocking over a glass of water. I came round lying on the floor, to hear my mother say, 'I feared as much.'

That faint was the first of many. At the mention of blood, I put my fingers in my ears. I began to look in the books we were to read aloud in school, to anticipate any references to blood. Then I asked to leave the room, and stayed out until I felt sure the dreaded passage was read. It is hard for others to understand the secret agony this phobia inspired. Blood was something talked about: poverty and disease surrounded us. My mother gave what little help she could.

'Give's a penny, for the love of Mary.'

Mother looked at the woman holding out her hand. She had a baby a few weeks old in her arms. The baby was covered by a ragged plaid shawl; clinging to her red skirt on each side were two small children. The boy of about three had nothing on but a dirty cream homespun petticoat-like garment. It reached half-way down his legs. Poor boys did not wear trousers until they were about twelve. The other child, a girl, could just walk, she was perhaps eighteen months old. She had on a dirty pink silk dress, no doubt someone's discarded party frock, which was much too big for her; her face was covered in sores. The mother and children were barefooted.

Mother opened her purse and took out sixpence. It was quite a lot of money. 'I don't like begging, but here you are. If you come up to the house tomorrow morning, I might find you a few things for the children.'

' 'Tis the kind lady ye are! May your shadow never grow less. May Mary, Joseph and all the saints bless you.'

Incidents like this made me aware that poverty, a low standard of living, disease and death were the lot of many who lived in the thatched cottages near us.

One morning, on my way to school, I saw a small coffin outside one of the cottages. It was leaning against the wall beside the door.

'Mother,' I said, when I got home, 'I saw a coffin outside the Flynns' door.'

'I know. Maureen died last night. I'm afraid Kathleen will soon follow her sister. It'll be a great day when they discover a cure for consumption.'

A month later, once again, there was a coffin leaning against the wall of the same cottage. I did not need to ask whose it was. Maureen was sixteen. Kathleen was fourteen. Death of the young in the West of Ireland was almost commonplace and accepted with resignation as the inscrutable will of God.

We read a poem of Matthew Arnold's in school. It seemed to me to sum up life – full of tragedy:

And we are here as on a darkling plain
Swept with confused alarms of struggle and flight,
Where ignorant armies clash by night.

One day I was looking over the bridge on the river. The water was flowing smooth and deep and calm. It almost seemed to beckon me, weighed down as I was by the sense of tears in mortal things. One plunge, and it would all be over, I thought. But I hadn't the courage.

The stresses of growing up often turn a girl's thoughts to introspection and morbidity. Yet my own religious quest had started much earlier. I was about five and a half when my mother asked: 'What ever are you doing?'

I was standing on a Victorian chair with a round padded back. I was leaning over the back, waving my hands about and speaking gibberish.

'I'm preaching,' I said. 'When I grow up, I'm going to be a preacher like grandpa.'

This grandpa, a minister in what is now the United Reformed Church, had just visited us. I heard him preach. I didn't understand a word of what he said. It didn't matter. It was *my* grandpa, tall, grey-headed, grey-bearded, dressed in a black gown with freshly-laundered linen bands, who was standing in that high oak pulpit. Every now and then he waved his hand. I thought he was waving at me and waved back.

'When you grow up,' my mother replied, 'you'll be a woman, and women are not allowed to preach.' It was my first dim realisation of what being a woman and not a man was going to mean when I grew up.

The religious dimension dominated the lives of most Irish people, whether Protestant or Catholic. There were a few sceptics about, such as my father.

'I had too much religion when young,' he often said.

But sceptics had little influence. Religion was the one consolation in a region where poverty, disease and early death were prevalent.

Up to a point, religion was a keeping of rules, a way of

escaping hell and gaining heaven after death. It must, however, be said that there were many devout men and women whose upright, self-sacrificing lives were a witness to their religious faith. For Roman Catholics, the main rule, which was almost universally observed, was to hear Mass on Sunday. On a Sunday, the Chapels were packed to overflowing. It was not uncommon to see quite a large crowd kneeling at the entrance because not another person was able to get into the building.

For Protestants, the rules were very different.

'What is the Fourth Commandment?' Regularly, we learnt, and were heard repeating, our Shorter Catechism. From the age of seven, I knew the answer: *Six days shalt thou labour and do all thy work: the seventh is the Sabbath of the Lord thy God. In it thou shalt not do any manner of work.*

This commandment was rigorously kept by the Protestant community, and particularly by Presbyterians. Only essential work was done on a Sunday. No knitting, sewing, games or homework were allowed. Once my sister and I were visiting my grandfather in Ballinasloe. He was a Scot, a strict Sabbatarian. His house, on a hill, overlooked the Fair Green. One Sunday afternoon, the Roman Catholics were playing games and running races. I found that by standing on a chair, I could see what was going on. Suddenly, my grandfather stood beside me and looked out. 'Ye'll na' break the Sabbath in my house,' he said, and pulled down the blind.

It was this Calvinist type of religion, rigid, dominated by the Protestant ethic, that was presented to me from my earliest days. From the sectarian point of view, there were 'them' and 'us'. 'Them' were the Roman Catholics. There was considerable religious tolerance in my parents. Nonetheless, in some insidious way, we soon learnt almost to despise Roman Catholics.

Over the back wall of the garden in Ballinasloe, we exchanged sectarian greetings. This activity was strictly forbidden, but it had a strange fascination. It was possible to climb far enough up the ivy-covered wall to be able to look down on the community on the other side, in Tea Lane. Immediately below us was a group of whitewashed thatched cottages, each with a stable-like door and windows only about eighteen inches square. Many of the cottages had not even a cold-water tap and used the communal tap in the street.

The people were very poor. A man in work might earn, at the most, six shillings a week. Many had no work. The families were large: eight to ten children in a family was common.

When our heads appeared over the wall, a group of children gathered. Their clothes were of the shabbiest, often ragged. Most were barefooted. Many had hair tangled by scratching, a sure sign of lice. Head lice were very common and catching. (At least once a week we had our long hair fine-combed!) A couple of older girls usually led the group. Each had two or three small brothers or sisters clinging to her dress. Led by these older children, the chanting began:

Protestant, Protestant, quack, quack, quack,
Go to the divil and never come back.

To this the reply was:

Saint Patrick's Day, we'll be merry and gay.
We'll murder the Catholics out of the way.
We'll drive them asunder, and make them lie under
The Protestant drum.

I often wonder where, at the age of seven, I picked up such an appalling rhyme. There was no direct teaching of sectarianism. In fact, most adults, no matter what their religious beliefs, lived peaceably and tolerantly with their neighbours. The sectarianism was passed on by children, unaware of its meaning or implications. Later on we learnt another rhyme, this time connected with the Bill for Home Rule for Ireland.

Sir Edward Carson had a cat that sat upon a stool,
And every time it caught a rat,
It shouted, 'No Home Rule!'
Sir Edward Carson had a cat without an ear.
And every time it caught a rat
It shouted, 'No Pope here!'

'How do we know we're right and the Pope's wrong?' I asked mother.

'Oh, you're too young to bother your head about such things,' she replied. I was then about twelve. This was the usual reply to many of my questions. But from this reply, I did gain a certain insight to the possibility of getting an answer. Something I had been told I was too young to understand, did in fact become quite clear a few months later. 'If I wait until I'm older, I'll understand,' became part of my philosophy of life.

But it was not so with religious belief. The older I got, the more puzzling and confusing it became. No one suggested that there was myth and legend in the Bible, so I took everything quite literally. This led to intellectual difficulties. 'You are not musical,' I was told, after unsuccessful attempts to get my small hands to stretch an octave on the piano. However then would I manage to play a golden harp even if I got to heaven? Because of my very fine hair, my hat was always askew. Could I keep the golden crown straight? Getting to heaven was indeed a remote possibility. Hell was much more likely. I knew *Line upon Line*, a current book of religious instruction, almost by heart. It said:

> Satan is glad
> When I am bad:
> And hopes that I
> With him will lie
> In fire and chains
> And dreadful pains.

I touched the hot range in the kitchen to feel what hell-fire was like. For a few hours afterwards, I behaved very well.

When I was about twelve, I was on a visit to my maternal grandfather. He gave me a book to read called *Faith and Assurance*. From it, difficult though it was, I gathered that, if you didn't know you were saved, you were damned. How did you *know*?

The minister came to see grandpa.

'I've given Frances your book to read,' grandpa told him.

The minister looked surprised. 'I think she's a bit too young for that. I've brought something more suitable for her.' Out of his pocket, he took a large orange and gave it to me.

Little did he guess that I had tried to read the book and was much bothered by it. I was far too shy to admit my interest, especially as, once again, I was said to be 'too young'.

As time went on and my mind developed, so did doubts and scepticism. The climax came in a Bible class. This was being conducted by a learned professor of the classics. The passage for our study was from the Book of Revelation, chapter six. 'Your turn to read,' the professor nodded to me.

'And I heard the number of those who had received the seal. From all the tribes of Israel there were a hundred and forty-four thousand.'

'Yes,' the professor went on, 'that is the number to be saved according to this text. Another Greek text reads, "Four thousand and forty-four".'

My heart sank. One hundred and forty-four thousand saved, or possibly only four thousand and forty-four. What chance was there for me? I had just learnt in mathematics about the Law of Probabilities. I did a sum. I found out the population of Ireland, multiplied it by 1916, and applied to this huge number the Law of Probabilities. The answer I got convinced me there was not the slightest chance for me. I might as well give up religion!

That was not so easily done. Alongside this intellectual religious quest, there ran another element, what I may call, 'a sense of the numinous'. This sense goes back as far as I can remember. It was easily called up. The darkness and subdued light in the forbidden Roman Catholic chapel gave me this sense. So did the gules of light through its stained-glass windows.

One day, in the garden, I came across a spider's web. It was suspended between two branches of the apple tree. The drops of dew glistened in the morning sun on the delicately-spun silver thread. The wonder of it held me spellbound. I was suddenly aware of some sort of 'otherness'. I was under eight at the time. I loved the symmetry and colour of the tall trees in Garbally Park. Once, as I stood at the foot of an enormous oak tree, and looked up to catch a glimpse of the sky through its branches, I felt myself to be a very tiny speck of the universe.

When we moved to live by the sea, beautiful sunrises or sunsets gave me the same sense of awe and wonder. So did the purple hills of Clare, half-hidden in sea mist. Later, when I came to read Wordsworth, I felt I knew exactly what he meant by:

the sense sublime
Of something far more deeply interfused
Whose dwelling is the light of setting suns.

In spite of unresolved intellectual difficulties, this sense of being enfolded in something greater than I, sustained me in the years to come.

Some call it God: some call it Love.

I hope they are one and the same.

1915–16
'A terrible beauty is born'

'What ever has your father got in the trap?' said my mother, looking out of the kitchen window. We ran out to see. On the seat was a large sack.

'Help me get this sack into the kitchen,' he called. My father was often paid in kind – this was one of those occasions. The sack was full of white flour which, with sugar, had become a luxury in 1915. Otherwise, food was not scarce, and in that sense the war seemed very remote. My father, tall and strong in his tweed jacket and shining leather leggings, lifted one end of the sack. We took the other end and helped to carry it into the kitchen. Alas, it was infested with mice.

Conscription did not apply in Ireland. The Home Rule Bill, which should have been enacted in September 1914, had been postponed. Irishmen flocked to join the forces, to fight side by side with England for the freedom of small nations. They believed Ireland was one of these. Before the war ended over 40,000 Irishmen had been killed. Those who did not join up were often the object of scorn.

'Do you know Jimmy Bryant?' a friend, Mary Wyatt, asked.

'Yes – what about him?'

'He's a coward, he's not volunteering. Let's send him a white feather. Can you get one?'

That was easy. We had white wyandotte fowls. I got the feather. Mary posted it.

A few days later, I met Jimmy's sister, a medical student. 'Jimmy's terribly upset.'

'What ever for?'

'Someone's sent him a white feather. I wish I knew who it was – they'd have a bit of my tongue! What they don't know is that Jimmy volunteered and is cut up at being turned down. They say he has the beginnings of tuberculosis.'

I kept quiet, but was filled with horror and guilt because I had helped with the white feather.

'I can't think how anyone can worship God in that whitewashed barn.'

The remark was made by the history teacher at school. She was a Roman Catholic. She was referring to the Presbyterian Church next door. She was somewhat scornful of Protestant ways, and particularly of Protestant-biased history books. Nevertheless, she gave us a fairly objective view of Irish history. Her own politics were never defined, but I suspect she had Republican leanings.

'Now for your next essay. Write on "Poets are the unacknowledged legislators of the world".'

Goodness knows what I wrote, but out of it came a discussion of the current young Irish poets. Their work was just beginning to be published. Their influence was strong on the young.

'Now, there's Patrick Pearce,' said Miss O'Neill. 'I think he's the best of them. They're all out to free Ireland. They're not afraid to die – indeed, they all believe that without sacrifice of blood there'll be no freedom. Listen to this from Pearce: *'There are many things more horrible than bloodshed, and slavery is one of them.'*

It was difficult for a young Protestant to acknowledge British rule as slavery, but the kernel of the idea was put into my mind.

'Surely, it would be better to get everyone to agree on Home Rule?' I ventured.

'Possibly, if you could *get* them to agree. Can you ever see Carson agreeing, with his "No Pope here"?'

To that question there was only the answer, 'No', then as now.

I began to read the Irish poets. All had the same theme – the doctrine of blood sacrifice.

In all humility and awe, we recognise that of us as of mankind before Calvary, it may be truly said without the shedding of blood there is no redemption.

wrote Connolly. Joseph Plunkett echoed the same sentiment.

Praise God, if this my blood fulfils the doom,
When you, dark rose shall redden into bloom.

On paper, discussed in school, it all seemed heroic and idealistic, but remote from reality.

Meanwhile, every night, bands of the Irish Republican Brotherhood drilled in adjacent fields. No one bothered much about them. There was plenty of space in which to drill: they were remote from official interference.

'Get half a dozen herrings on your way back from school,' mother said. 'Here is the money.'

I dawdled and got down to the Claddagh just as the fish-market was closing. I went up to Mrs McHugh, a fish-woman we knew. She had on a voluminous hand-woven red skirt which reached to her ankles. A white linen apron was tied round her waist, and over it was a second canvas apron, somewhat bloodstained from gutting fish. A small black shawl was crossed on her ample bosom; a larger grey shawl with a patterned border rested on her shoulders. Her iron-grey hair was secured in a knot by large hairpins, gleaming because the black enamel had worn off them. Her feet were bare.

'Can I have six fresh herrings, please?'

'Sure,' she said as she began to wrap the fish in newspaper. Then she paused and pointed to the fish left in her basket. 'Will you have the last few?'

'Sorry, they would be too many. Anyway, I haven't any more money.'

She gave me the parcel of fish, turned from me and held up two silver herrings with navy-blue markings, red-gilled and still stiff.

'Two fresh herrings for three ha'pence,' she offered. No one wanted the fish, so she threw them into the flat willow fish basket and put it on her head.

Mrs O'Donnelly came across the market-place, now nearly empty.

'Oh is yourself going? I'll come with you,' she said. The two women started to walk, heads erect to keep the baskets steady. Pushing my bicycle over the cobbles I walked with them.

'I'm worried about my Paddy,' Mrs O'Donnelly confided. 'He's after joining the 'IRB.'

'What's this IRB?'

'Irish Republican Brotherhood. It's run by them clever ones in Dublin. Paddy says they're poets.'

'Ah now, if they're poets I don't expect there's much harm in it. It'll keep him out of mischief.'

'I'm not so sure. Hasn't he got a gun hidden in the rafters? An' he creeps out at night for drillin'. Can't wake him in the morning to get the cow milked.'

In Main Street our ways parted so I did not hear any more.

It was Easter Monday, 1916. I was fifteen.

'I shan't be going,' said my mother, who was busy weeding the flower-bed. 'There's going to be thunder above or below before the day is out.'

This was the answer I got to my question: 'Mother, when are you going to pack?'

My parents were to go to Dublin on the Tuesday for the Fairy House Races. My father was to be one of the veterinary surgeons in attendance. For the first time in my life, I, the eldest of five, was to be 'in charge'. I was most anxious to assume my responsibilities. Hence my eager question. I can feel, even after all these years, the sense of foreboding my mother's answer gave me.

It was a close, clammy afternoon, following a very wet morning. My younger brother and I were standing in front of Wellpark which was on a slight hill and overlooked Galway Bay. It was because of this situation that we were to be so involved in the dramatic events of the next few days.

My mother was right. She was a mixture of Irish and Scottish. She had, at times, the uncanny second sight of the Celt. I do not remember whether any thunder occurred in the heavens, but by the evening her prognostications of thunder below were well confirmed.

My father was on a case in a town up the line. He was expected on the nine o'clock train. He did not come in until eleven o'clock.

'There's a rising in Dublin,' he said. 'We can't go tomorrow.'

In Dublin, a few hundred men of the IRB were attempting to defy the might of England. For four days they held out. Failure of communication meant that there was little support in other parts of the country. County Galway was one of the exceptions.

The week after the Rising, my mother had a letter from my uncle in England.

'Your uncle wants you to write an account of what happened last week. You'd better do it this morning.'

It was a lovely day. I didn't want to settle down to writing under compulsion.

'I haven't any paper.'

'Look in the drawer in the sideboard. There's a pad of blue writing paper there. That'll do. Now, go and get it done in time for the post.'

So reluctantly, I got the blue-lined paper and wrote down some of the things that had happened in Galway during the week of the Rising. Somewhat yellowed and faded, its pages fastened together with a rusty safety-pin, it has survived. That I tired of writing it is clear from the deterioration in my handwriting.

DIARY OF EASTER WEEK, 1916
Monday, 24 April 1916
Easter Monday was a pouring wet day and passed quietly until the evening when the usual 9.00 pm train did not come in. This caused some excitement, but at about 10.30 pm a special came from Mullingar bringing passengers from the intermediate stations. With it came the news that the Sinn Feiners had risen in Dublin and killed many people. Pappie, who was at Oranmore, the next station, came on this special.

Tuesday
There was great excitement in Galway on Tuesday, for the news had arrived that the Sinn Feiners had seized the village of Oranmore. The police were very active and two [English] cruisers came into the Roads [Galway Bay]. Commander Hannon issued an order that all public houses were to be shut and people were to remain indoors from 5.00 pm to 8.00 am.

Wednesday
Wednesday was the most eventful day of the week in Galway. The Sinn Feiners had reached Carnmore, about four miles outside Galway. At 5.30 am the police went out to meet them and an engagement took place. The Sinn Feiners fled but not without killing one constable. The rebels deny that any of their men were killed, but it is reported that there were three.

About ten o'clock we noticed police round different fields. At about 11.30 we started for town, but met a body of police and were told that the Sinn Feiners were coming down past Wellpark to seize Galway. We hurried home and kept watch for about an hour. Suddenly, and without warning, we heard a loud report. It was a shell from one of the cruisers in the Bay. More shots were fired until about ten had found their mark. Some fell just behind Wellpark, but the only damage known to be done was the killing of a cow, and of course many large holes. Later we learnt that two of the shells went right over our house. After the bombarding things became quieter and after tea we went to town. Everyone seemed surprised to see us, and seemed to think our house had been captured. Another story was that we had 40 marines and two machine guns in the house.

When we came home we saw searchlights and were sent word from the commander to keep lights in the front windows, as they would be a guide to the vessels. There were many rumours that Athenry [twelve miles from Galway] would be bombarded. We slept in our schoolroom, and there were about three faint shots.

Thursday
On Thursday many fears were allayed by the arrival of a warship. It was the *Gloucester* which sunk the *Goeben*. Many troops were landed from this vessel and another troopship, and sentries were posted to prevent provisions going into the country. It was awfully funny to see soldiers prodding [loads of] seaweed etc.

Friday
On Friday the yeast in the town ran short and so did butter, and many did without either. Upwards of 300 prisoners were brought in in motors.

The next week things became more as usual and supplies of yeast arrived.

Within a fortnight of the Rising an Irishwoman wrote: *It's like wading through a river of blood under a closed door.*

She was speaking of the executions that followed. An execution in Ireland was a source of ghoulish glee. The last night of a condemned man was reported in every detail: what he ate, how much he slept, who visited him, the amount of brandy he was given as he was led from the death cell to the scaffold. I used to spend sleepless nights in agony before every execution in Galway jail, putting myself in the place of the condemned man. It was a great relief when I heard the clock strike eight and knew that it was all over.

So it was with the executions after the Rising. I lay awake imagining what it was like to be about to be shot. I knew I had not the courage to face such an ordeal. It was no use saying to myself, *You're most unlikely to be condemned to death.* I think the execution of Edith Cavell brought it within the realms of possibility.

The *Irish Times* was delivered to our house early. I often had a look at it before breakfast. I began to dread its arrival. Day after day it told of further executions, often in great detail. Much as I hated to read about these executions, I could not help doing so: I was abhorred but at the same time fascinated by them. I discovered that the last nights of those about to be shot were very different from what I imagined. Each felt he was dying for the sake of Ireland and freedom.

'It looks as if the executions are at an end,' said my father a week later, looking up from his reading of the *Irish Times*.

'I see the death sentence on de Valera has been commuted. It's about time too. All the leading Sinn Feiners have been wiped out. Any more executions will look like vengeance.'

'There's Connolly left,' my mother said.

'True, but I hear he's in a bad way. He can't walk – his ankle is shattered and he has other injuries. No one would shoot a man in that state!'

What was generally considered impossible happened, as I learnt from my reading of the *Irish Times* the next day.

Early in the morning of 11 May, the prison chaplain was fetched. 'I was astonished,' he said, 'I felt sure there would be no more executions.'

According to the account, Connolly was carried on a stretcher to the jail yard, and put on a chair.

'Will you pray for the men who are about to shoot you?' asked the priest.

'I will say a prayer for all brave men who do their duty,' he replied.

'Father, forgive them, for they know not what they do,' were his last words.

Connolly's execution was indeed the last. It brought the number executed to fifteen in nine days.

1916–18
'Will YOU answer the call?'

The war between England and Germany dragged on. Men were urgently needed. Large recruiting posters appeared in all sorts of places in Galway. Even the horse-drawn trams displayed them.

The poster showed a red-haired girl in a white robe half covered by a blue cloak. She was playing an Irish harp through the strings of which was seen a British Tommy blowing a bugle. A succession of musical notes issued from the bugle. Presumably they were the music to the title of the poster: 'Will YOU answer the call?' Underneath the picture was written in capital letters, NOW IS THE TIME. Yet a little lower down was the direction: *And the place is the nearest recruiting office.*

A letter to my grandfather at that time shows that the recruiting drive met with little response.

> Only 45 recruits have joined the army since June. 2,900 must be obtained by October. There will be a large clock to tell the no. of recruits obtained, erected in Eyre Square.

The message of the poster was reinforced by the Royal Flying Corps as I say in the same letter:

> We see scores of aeroplanes now. We do not even bother to look at them. They do all sorts of turns and twists and drop recruiting papers over the town.

Conscription was being enforced in England. The threat of it hung over Ireland. It was much resented, especially among the Catholics, though thousands of them joined up. Protestants, on the whole, supported England. The casualties were very high.

One lovely June day in 1916, I was passing the gates of the Erasmus Smith Grammar School. A tall young man in a Second Lieutenant's uniform came out. I knew James Stewart, but was shy about speaking to one so exalted.

'Hello,' he said, 'how goes it?'

'All right. Where are you off to?'

'I'm for France tonight. I've just been in to see the old show.'
He walked with me as far as the station. 'So long now!' he said.

The tall figure disappeared into the station.

About a week later I said to my mother: 'Everywhere I go, I seem to see James Stewart.'

'Are you tarred with this brush too?' she replied.

'What brush?'

'Well, we've got Highland blood in our veins. Sometimes we get a sort of second sight.'

I forgot about James for a few days. Then one day my father came in late for the midday meal.

'I'm late because I've just heard some very bad news. James Stewart was killed in the Battle of the Somme.'

He had died on the day I kept seeing him.

Materially, the war affected us comparatively little. Food was not really short. Occasionally, there was a rumour of a submarine in Galway Bay. Otherwise, life went on at its leisurely pace, with one exception. The pressure on men, particularly those of the Protestant community, to join the forces increased. My father volunteered for the Royal Veterinary Corps, and was soon sent to France. In the autumn of 1918, he came home for a week's leave. He had been home two days when a telegraph boy rang the bell. Telegrams were commonplace in our household as there was no telephone. Delia, the current maid, brought the telegram to my mother. She began to open the envelope.

'Oh dear,' she said, 'I suppose the news has got round he's home. I hope he hasn't got to go far.'

She read the telegram. Without a word she went into the garden where my father was working, and handed the telegram to him. I was watching through the window. They spoke together for a moment or two. Then my father took the fork out of the ground and went to put it in the shed.

Mother came in.

'Has Dad got to go on a case?' I asked.

'It's worse than that. He's got to go back to France immediately.' She handed me the telegram. It read: 'Leave cancelled. Rejoin unit at once.'

We all walked down to the station to see him off on the boat train. Had he been allowed to stay his full leave he would have been on the *Leinster*, the mail-boat sunk by a German submarine a few days later.

My mother wrote to him soon after:

Very great grief was expressed here at your sudden departure and many prayers were uttered for the ending of the war. Why? That you would soon be back to save their cattle for them! You are 'a most terrible loss to the country!' I think it is most highly flattering to you. Your return to Connaught is considered more important than President Wilson's peace terms!

As fewer and fewer Irishmen volunteered for the British forces, the threat of conscription increased. The new nationalist movement led by de Valera, under the old name of Sinn Fein, was rapidly gaining ground, particularly in the west. On the whole, the movement had until now condemned the 1916 Rising and supported the Home Rule party.

It was against this background that I spent my last years at school. An ethos of hard work meant that we passed the required examinations without undue bother. However, there was not a girl in the school who had not a relative in the British forces. Hardly a week passed without news of a casualty, a brother, a cousin, an older sister's fiancé, or a friend.

It was early in 1918. I was hard at work in the little study at school. The Headmistress looked in. She had two little girls with her.

'Frances,' she said, 'here are Anne and Nu. Will you look after them for a while? Take them into the garden.'

As I took the two little girls out, I saw that the Headmistress was deep in conversation with Lady Gregory, the distinguished Irish writer. She had on a long black dress over which she wore a short bulky black coat. A flat black hat sat on her head like a pancake, and on her wrist hung a large black reticule. I remembered the reticule. Once on a train journey with my mother, she had given me a sweet from it.

'That's my grandma,' Anne informed me. We played outside for a while, until Lady Gregory came over to us. She gave me a gracious nod, as she led the two little girls away.

I soon found out the significance of her visit. She had just received word that her only son, Major Robert Gregory, had been killed in an air battle in Italy.

In Yeats's poem 'An Irishman foresees his death', he is the airman.

> I know that I shall meet my fate
> Somewhere among the clouds above . . .

> . . . Nor law nor duty bade me fight
> Nor public men nor cheering crowds.
> A lonely impulse of delight
> Drove to this tumult in the clouds.

Amid all the turmoil of the First World War, with its seemingly endless toll of young life: amid my increasing awareness of the political unrest in Ireland, one centre, the home, held. The very solidity of the walls of most of the homes, whether cottage or castle, gave a sense of the security within.

In our home, on weekdays the daily routine was very strict. We dare not, for instance, be late for a meal. Immediately after tea, we all settled down to do our homework. There was a room called the 'schoolroom' set aside for us. A large scrubbed kitchen table stood in the middle of the room. Bookshelves lined two of the walls. They contained a miscellaneous collection of books – Greek, Latin and Hebrew textbooks, Victorian classic fiction, books on birds, books on wild flowers, and a big shelf of *Boys' Own Papers* dated in the 1880s. These were no doubt the relics of my mother's four brothers. This collection of books was to direct my own reading, and account for an extraordinary miscellaneous general knowledge. I found Foxe's *Book of Martyrs*, and read it with a mixture of horror and fascination. A book in a soft green suede cover attracted my attention. *The Crown of Wild Olive* was the title. 'What a lovely title,' I thought. I took it down and, curled up on the window seat, settled down for a good read. The sense of disappointment and frustration is with me still, when I found that it was, at least to me, a very dry book on architecture.

Mother sat at one end of the table. Usually she was darning. The youngest, learning to read, sat beside her. When the child lost her place, mother pointed out the right word with her darning needle. As we learnt our poetry or tables or history dates, mother heard them. Not until we were word-perfect were we allowed to get down. One hesitation, one wrong word, brought the reprimand, 'No, you haven't learnt that properly. Do it again.'

Homework finished, books were carefully put away. I was untidy and lazy. Again and again, I left my books scattered on the table as I was usually the last to leave. Then one night, I was taught a lesson I never forgot. Mother was shaking me awake.

'Come on,' she said, 'get on your slippers. Your books are all over the place again. This time, you'll put them away.'

Sleepily, I stumbled down the stairs to the schoolroom. 'Now look at your composition,' she said.

I had left my composition for the next day lying exposed on the table. It was my favourite subject. I had spent much time and care on it. The clean white page was all smeared with a yellowish substance. 'It serves you right,' said mother.

When homework was finished, my brother blew a bird's egg somewhat inexpertly. The contents had landed on my clean page!

Until my father joined up in 1918, Sunday afternoon was the loveliest time of all the week. Immediately after the midday dinner, we all went to the drawing-room. The fire was lit and welcoming. Only on Sundays were we allowed in that room.

Before we had settled down, there was always a knock on the door. 'Come in.'

Delia's head peeped round the door. 'I'm off now, ma'am. The tea's laid.'

'Thank you, Delia. Be sure you're in by ten. And be careful on the way home.'

'Ah shure, me cousin Tom'll see me home.'

The door closed. My mother and father exchanged glances. Mother smiled. 'Considering she's a country girl from Connemara, it's amazing how many cousins she's got in Galway.'

My father sat on one side of the fireplace, in the big armchair, my mother, the opposite side, in what was called 'the lady's chair'. The five of us scrambled for the settee, or sat on the warm Wilton rug. It was indeed a scene of peace. Subdued light from two paraffin lamps was reflected in the highly-polished brass. The marble fireplace had a large brass canopy embossed with a design of opening flowers, which I always thought were tulips. Two brass firedogs supported brass fire-irons, a poker, a pair of tongs and a fire shovel. The rectangular fender, also of brass, was about eighteen inches high. At each corner was a nymph, poised on one foot. Inside the fender was a pile of turf sods. Beside the fender, neatly stacked, was another pile of firewood, logs cut from the many trees that blew down in the gales. The gentle light from the lamps seemed to give a rosier sheen to the furniture in the room. The furniture was all antique. It was, even before antiques became popular, the envy of many of our friends.

'Where ever did you get that lovely table?' Mrs Woods pointed to a rosewood table by the window.

'At Lord Butler's auction. I was lucky, hardly anyone was bidding. I got it for fifteen shillings. I got most of the other things too. It's much cheaper than the new stuff.'

Mother loved auctions. At the time there were many of them. The owners of large houses, fearful of the unstable political situation, were selling up and moving to England. Mother had a real eye for a bargain. Occasionally, she took a gamble on a job lot, a box of miscellaneous items, odds and ends put together by the auctioneer at the end of a sale. The price was usually half-a-crown. The box might contain just a collection of rubbish, cracked cups and the like. However, mother was often fortunate and got some very nice bits of silver and china.

The three large windows of the drawing-room had mahogany shutters which were pulled up from a narrow rectangular well beneath them. Often the windows shuddered in a particularly fierce blast from the Atlantic Ocean, winds which were very common in the West of Ireland. The booming from the lighthouse was always the sign that the west wind was fierce and strong. Then the whole house swayed as the blasts of wind hit it. The drawing-room seemed all the more warm and secure.

We knew that there was a war on in Europe. We knew it was possible that by the middle of the week, news might come of the death in France of yet another local young man. We knew that acts of violence happened almost daily all round us. But we were growing up with violence. It had become a part of life. We took it in our stride. The peace of Sunday was seldom disturbed.

Protestants did not visit on Sunday, except by invitation. For Roman Catholics, it was a real day of relaxation. Games of camogie, a form of hurling, or a football match, or drilling in some remote place absorbed the energies of young rebels.

We all settled down to read. Mother read to the younger two, often a story from the Old Testament. The rest of us read stories of our own choice, usually selected from the miscellaneous collection that formed our home library. Among them were *Uncle Tom's Cabin*, *Little Women*, and the stories of Jack London.

As I got older, I went 'poetry-mad', and read a good deal of the poetry of Wordsworth, Browning and Tennyson. I was particularly fond of Tennyson. Not so my sister. One day in the school cloakroom, I was passing on a bit of information to a select few. I did not want it to be made public, so I said: 'Tell it not in Gath, publish it not in the streets of Askelon.' Bible quotations came easily.

'There's she at her everlasting Tennyson,' remarked my sister.

As we read, often there was silence for a long time, broken only by the turning of a page, or a sighing from the fire as a log subsided. Every now and then, my father put another log on the fire, took down the bag of sweets from the mantelpiece and said: 'Who'd like another sweet?' There was a chorus of 'me please.' He threw a sweet to each of us. We were experts at catching. The bag went round four or five times.

Occasionally, there was a loud knock on the front door. Mother paused in her reading. 'Now, who ever's that on a Sunday afternoon?'

'I'll see.'

My father always answered the door himself if a knock came at an unusual time. There was a certain feeling of unease. We all listened. Voices were heard. Then the front door closed.

'Just sit down a few minutes, while I get my bag,' we heard my father say. The tension eased. We went back to our books. My father came back.

'Milk fever case,' he said. 'Moycullen. Don't wait tea.' Immediately, there was a cry of 'bags', as we rushed to get his chair.

At six o'clock there was Sunday tea in the dining-room. An Irish linen damask cloth, shining and smooth from much ironing, covered the big mahogany table. The design of shamrocks, thistles and oak leaves seemed almost to be raised. There was plenty of bread and butter, home-made jam, scones and one piece of plum cake each. The cups were Coalport, white with gold handles. Mother had them for a wedding present. She did not like them, so they were relegated to second-best.

Teatime was the culmination of Sunday. Immediately afterwards, the younger ones went to bed. We older ones might sing hymns for half an hour, to mother's accompaniment. By eight o'clock we were all in bed.

How wise the Old Testament Jews were, and how good their psychology, when they insisted on the keeping of the Sabbath rest! That day a week, freed from the ordinary work and routine of the other six, meant that we started back to work on Monday morning, relaxed and refreshed. I, for one, never knew what was meant by the 'Monday morning feeling'.

The postman pushed a large heavy packet through the letter-box. It fell with a thud on the tiled hall floor.

'Mother, mother, Swan and Edgar's catalogue has come! Are we having something new?'

'We'll have to see,' said mother.

We had few new clothes. What we had were very carefully looked after. To school, we wore navy-blue skirts, and a white blouse or jumper. As soon as we got home, the first thing was to change into play clothes, the cast-offs of the years before. Sunday clothes were kept for Sunday, or special occasions. My mother had a flair for dress. Not only was she always smart, she provided clothes for my sister and myself which raised envious eyebrows and even the comment, 'How extravagant!' In fact, very little was spent on dress. The secret was Swan and Edgar's, Piccadilly, London, S.W.1. How well I knew the address! (When I saw the last shutter go up on the shop in 1980, I felt sadness and nostalgia. It had given so much pleasure to two little girls in the West of Ireland, seventy years before.)

What poring over that catalogue there was! Mother put a neat pencil mark by a possible frock or coat. We soon learnt what was too expensive for her tick. Then she wrote to Swan and Edgar, requesting certain articles on approval. Often by return of post, a large dress box, or sometimes two, marked 'On Approval' was delivered.

'No looking until after tea,' mother said.

Then, with carefully-washed hands, and in clean petticoats, we met in mother's room. The one long mirror in the house was there. Carefully, the layers of tissue paper were unfolded and the frocks laid out on the bed. One by one we tried them on. There was only a year between my sister and myself. As she was of a slightly bigger build, we were often taken for twins, especially as we wore almost identical clothes. The only difference was that I always had blue trimmings and hair ribbons, my sister, pink.

'What a pity they haven't sent one with a blue border!' Mother was looking at a frock with a pink border.

'This is quite the nicest, and will wash well.'

I had my eyes on the frock with a mauve pattern. I loved mauve. 'Couldn't I have this one?'

'No, mauve's too old for you.'

I tried on the frock.

'Well,' said mother, turning me round, 'it's very nice and it's time you began to choose for yourself. You really like it?'

I did and, for the first time, I had a frock of my own choosing and not identical with my sister's.

The Armistice came at last. It was signed on the eleventh day of the eleventh month of 1918. There were no radios in those days, but somehow the news reached Galway.

We were given a holiday from school immediately. It seemed right to celebrate a British victory. But little had we gauged the local popular mood.

I went into a shop on my way home. 'Can I have a yard of red, white and blue ribbon, please?'

'I'll not sell you any such thing,' said the shop assistant, to my amazement. She turned her back on me.

I got the ribbon in a bigger shop and, displaying a large bow, began to cycle the mile home. I had to get off on the hill in Bohermore.

Suddenly, I was soused with a bucket of dirty suds. A woman shouted: 'Take that, you Orange dog.' I stood still and looked at my soaked skirt. Water, tinged with navy dye, was dripping into my shoes. My first thought was: *Goodness, it's my best school skirt.* Then I looked across at the woman standing in the doorway of a cottage. The empty zinc bucket was still swinging in her hand. She was shaking her fist at me. I caught something about, 'the damned British', and 'my Paddy tortured in prison'.

Bewildered, I made no reply, but got on my bicycle, and pedalled down the hill home.

'Don't tell me that is about here,' said my mother when I showed her my soaked skirt. 'I am more than sorry.'

'But why should she call me an Orange dog?'

'Well, she knows your father is in the British army. She knows we are Protestants. I suppose she thinks all Protestants are Orangemen. I can't blame her. The Orange Order is very bitter against Catholics.'

I had vaguely heard of Orange Parades on 12 July. Our history lessons had taught us that they were to celebrate the defeat by William of Orange of James II in 1690. These parades were confined to Ulster and I had never come across an Orangeman. The incident was another pointer towards the deep-seated suspicion that existed between Catholic and Protestant.

We children found a Union Jack and hoisted it through an attic window in the roof of the house.

That evening, we were sitting quietly in the dining-room. The lamps were lit: the curtains were undrawn. Suddenly there came the sound of breaking glass. Stones were being showered into the long passage outside the dining-room. Quick as lightning, my mother extinguished the lamps, and drew the curtains. Risking a flying stone, she went round the house putting out all the lights. There was just the one fusillade of stones. After that all went quiet. For the first time, we put up the shutters and locked the outside doors.

Though I did not realise it then, it was the shape of things to come.

1918–20
Sunt lacrimae rerum –
'There is a sense of tears in things'

It was the end of November, 1918. My father was still in France although the war was at last over. 'I want to show you something,' said my mother.

She took me to the long first-floor passage in our house. In it was a large oak linen press. Mother opened the cupboard. From the top shelf, she took down a set of Irish linen sheets and pillowcases. They had been freshly laundered, and smelt of orris-root.

'We can't all live for ever,' she said. 'If anyone dies, these are for the laying-out. It saves a lot of trouble if someone knows about them.'

She put the linen back on the top shelf and carefully covered it with an old clean sheet.

'Another thing,' she went on, 'if you have to deal with a death alone, there are a few things that are immediately important. Stretch out the limbs. Tie a big handkerchief round the chin and round the head. That keeps the mouth shut. Then close the eyes and put pennies on them.'

My mother's second sight was almost uncanny.

Almost the only form of public entertainment in Galway was 'the pictures'. We often had complimentary tickets, very probably my father's payment for professional services to some animal. Mother took a sister and a brother to see *My Four Years in Germany*. I was revising for an examination and stayed at home. The date was 2 December, a Monday. On the following day mother developed a feverish cold. She seemed so poorly that, next day, I called the doctor on my way to school. He told her to stay in bed until the following Monday. She had caught the Spanish flu. My younger brother also got the flu, but fortunately mildly.

On Saturday morning, I too had a cold and developed a bad headache. In the evening, I went in to see mother. She was reading *The Greatest Thing in the World*, by Henry Drummond.

'I think I've got the flu,' I said.

'Now don't imagine things, Frances. Go down and get the boys' socks darned.' This was my Saturday night task. I took out the thick grey woollen socks, knee-length with the scarlet school stripe round the top. Somehow I cobbled up the holes and then went to bed. Elizabeth, who was a year younger, had already had the flu. She was left to cope with the three of us.

The doctor came daily. My brother recovered quickly but my mother and I were very ill.

On the Monday, the doctor came into my room. 'I think I ought to warn you that your mother is very ill,' he said. 'She has developed double pneumonia.'

'Couldn't we get a specialist from Dublin?'

'It would be no use,' he said, 'I'm trying to get a nurse.' Nurses were scarce. The doctor found one who was nursing a family with scarlet fever. They were now convalescent and agreed to release the nurse. Her coming relieved my sister somewhat.

The days between between Monday and Wednesday are vague. I too had double pneumonia. I did know that an effort was being made to locate my father in France.

The doctor came twice on Tuesday evening. 'You must be prepared for the worst,' he said.

I was too ill to take in the implications of what he was saying. It was a sleepless night. I was coughing incessantly. I could hear my mother coughing occasionally. She was talking a lot. I heard the nurse call my sister at about two o'clock. My sister lay down on the sofa in the drawing-room next door to me. The night seemed endless. The nurse looked in occasionally.

'How's mother?' I asked each time. She pulled the door to and went out. A week later I wrote in a letter: *I felt awful lying helpless, but it was no use trying to get up and make things worse.*

About half-past six, I heard the nurse waken my sister. I called out, but there was no reply. Suddenly the dog began to howl, long-drawn-out wails. Then there was silence. It was broken from the outside. The yard gate banged. There was a certain amount of commotion, the crunching of heavy boots on the gravel, the thud of a stick on an animal's back, accompanied by 'Get on now, will ye!' It was Tom, our faithful man, taking the bullock to market as he had been instructed by mother.

As far as I was concerned, there was a conspiracy of silence, apparently on the doctor's orders. I knew my mother had died, but no one would confirm it. 'Had mother died?' I asked the nurse point-blank. She pushed the thermometer into my mouth. Maggie had come in with a cup of something. 'How's mother?' I asked her. She burst into tears, put down the cup and saucer, and fled. She went downstairs, stopped all the clocks, turned the chairs in the kitchen upside down, and retired to bed – not from flu but from fright! The brunt of everything now fell heavier on my sister.

At last the doctor came in to see me. 'How's mother?' I asked, really knowing the answer. He hesitated. 'Tell me the truth, I'm the eldest.'

He did. Later, I heard that he was surprised at my lack of emotion.

I found a Bible and rummaged until I found the bit in St John's Gospel where it says: *I am the resurrection, and the life*. It didn't help. Everything seemed very unreal. There was no word of my father, but friends rallied round.

'Shall we get a single plot or a double one in the graveyard?' I was asked. From my bed I was beginning to take control. The Scot in me came out.

'It's more economical to get a double plot,' I replied. 'It's sure to be needed sometime.' So a double plot it is, but mother lies in it alone.

'No one must come into the house unnecessarily,' the doctor said to me. 'This septic flu is very infectious. I'm going to lock the door of your mother's room and take the key as soon as she's coffined.' The coffin came that evening. The linen sheets were never used. No one else knew about them. Many people called at the door, but were not allowed in. They were deprived of the privilege dear to the Irish of 'viewing the corpse'.

My father's eldest brother came over from England on the Thursday. There was still no word of my father. At the insistence of the doctor, mother was buried on 13 December, the nineteenth anniversary of her wedding.

I had been moved into the drawing-room for warmth. Its large windows looked out on the hill leading to the cemetery. The nurse pulled the bed to a window. I looked on unmoved as the hearse mounted the hill. The horses, their thick black plumes fluttering, strained slightly under its weight. On the coffin were two wreaths of golden chrysanthemums. One was from us, one from the Grammar School. My younger sister, aged eight, stood beside me. She had on a black dress with a white collar. It had come from Swan and Edgar's only a fortnight before.

'I don't like black for a child,' mother had said, looking over the frocks on approval. 'Apparently it is impossible to get navy. At least it's practical. I'd better have it.'

My father had only received the first telegram sent to say mother was ill. He got compassionate leave immediately, but did not get home until Saturday, the day after the funeral.

At Oranmore, the next station to Galway, the station-master offered his condolences. 'It's dreadful losing the two of them,' he said. Rumour had it that I too had died. By the time my father got home, I was taking a turn for the better. According to the letter I wrote to my aunt, who was still with the forces in Malta, I had thirteen days in bed.

When I got up and about again, I had suddenly grown up. Life, even in my old age, is divided into two by my mother's death. It was ten years before I shed any tears. The Protestant ethic in which I had been brought up demanded the stiff upper lip.

I came across in Virgil's *Aeneid*, the line, *Sunt lacrimae rerum et mentem mortalia tangunt* (there is a sense of tears in things and mortals' sorrows touch the hearts).

At that time, it summed up everything.

'Who was to look after the five of us?' That was the immediate question that Christmas, 1918. My mother was the last of her family. Five younger brothers had died before her. Our only relative on her side was her father, then aged eighty-two. My father had three sisters, but none of them was free to come.

To me, the obvious thing was to leave school and look after the house. However, another solution seemed possible. I wrote to one of my aunts just before Christmas, 1918:

> I am quite prepared to give up school and do my best at home. Mother had taught me a good lot . . . but Pappie and Uncle Frank think it is a pity, when I have got so far. I think we're going to try to get a sort of housekeeper . . . I am quite delighted at the thought of going on with my work. There is one thing I know that I could not do, and that is do the housekeeping and lessons together . . . I should pity the house that had to get on with the spare time my lessons leave me.

'Frances, of all people, to look after a house!' was my aunt's comment. 'She'd never have her nose out of a book.' She got an early release from the army and came over to see us a couple of months later.

'I was never so surprised in my life,' she said, years later. 'Everything was going on much as usual.'

The housekeeper never came. No one wanted the job. My sister, a year younger, was most competent. We stayed on at school and managed the house between us, until she went over to England to train as a teacher.

I had passed the Irish Senior Grade Certificate, having credits in the right subjects to give me exemption from the entrance examination of Trinity College, Dublin, and most of the English universities, but it was now impossible to leave home. There was, however, a constituent college of the National University of Ireland in Galway. Part of the upsurge of nationalism in the early part of the century was the attempt to revive Gaelic, the native Irish language. Irish became compulsory for entrance to the National University.

'I think the best thing for you to do is to learn Irish and get the National University Matric,' advised my uncle. I was born on his birthday, and bore his names. He always showed much interest in my education. 'Is there an Irish teacher anywhere?'

'Yes, the maths teacher at school is a native Irish speaker. I know he teaches Irish at the Boys' Seminary.'

'Good, get him to give you lessons; I'll pay for them.'

Modern languages were not my strong point, but I was motivated. So, in February 1919, I started to learn Irish with a view to taking the Matriculation examination in June. I had to cycle five miles to have a lesson. I was too ambitious. I failed the June examination. Fortunately, there was another in September. My sister left school in July and took over the housekeeping.

For two months I did nothing but Irish. I plagued the local Irish speakers, but unfortunately none of them could write the language. I sat the examination again. Never have I waited for the results of an examination with such fear and trembling. *Would I pass? What could I do if I failed?* The results did not come.

In early October, two days before the term began, I signed up at the University, but I could not be admitted to lectures without that pass in Irish. Next morning, as I was getting the breakfast, I saw the postman come up the drive. Had he anything for me? I did not dare to go to meet him. Suddenly, I heard a thud on the tiled floor of the hall. Something rolled along the ground. I did not need to look. It was the cardboard container of the Irish Matriculation Certificate. A failure would have come in an envelope. I had passed! Never did an examination pass give me such pleasure and hope.

So my life for the next four years was divided between academic study and home economics. With my sister to share, we managed very well. At the time we had a competent maid. When Elizabeth went to England, there began the saga of domestic helps.

The competent maid left, attracted to England by higher wages and less work. I heard of another who was employed in an hotel. 'She's a wonderful worker, and a good cook,' said her employer Mrs Sheehy. 'I'm only sorry to lose her. She would like to be with older children.' She was keen to come, so I engaged her.

'One thing I ought to tell you,' said Mrs Sheehy as I was leaving, 'Norah had a baby when she was only fifteen. It was her employer's fault. But she's twenty-three now and has learnt her lesson.'

What a treasure Norah was! She was strong: she could cook: she could milk on occasion. I was in paradise. Life became very easy.

Then one day a friend of my mother's came to tea. Norah brought it in. 'How long have you had that maid?' asked Mrs Scott.

'About three months. She's marvellous.'

'She may be, but I'm sorry to tell you she's at least six months pregnant.'

My world was shattered. I wasn't used to asking a maid if she were pregnant. Anyway, I was too ignorant to notice her condition.

'Mrs Scott thinks you're having a baby,' I ventured.

'Yes, miss, she's right.'

'What are you going to do?'

'Stay here as long as you'll let me. Then it's the Magdalen.' The Magdalen was a laundry run by nuns who took in fallen girls. Life in it was not easy for them.

I had to tell my father. He didn't seem too surprised. 'She's very fit. Let her stay another two months,' he said.

'It would take a Protestant to do that,' commented the Parish Priest.

After that, older and more enlightened, I questioned would-be maids as closely as I dared. But two pregnant ones followed in succession. Each one departed without warning.

One of these, Mary, was very promising. She was married to a soldier in the Connaught Rangers. 'Is there any reason why you should not stay with us for at least a year?' I asked her when she came to see me.

'None at all, miss,' she replied. I thought she understood what I was really asking, so I hoped we were going to be settled for a while.

She helped me with the dinner on Christmas Day, was given her presents and the rest of the day off.

On Boxing Day when I went down to the kitchen, the fire was not lit, and there were no signs of preparation for breakfast. I thought she had overslept.

'Mary,' I called up the stairs. As I got no reply, I went up to her room. The door was open, the bed was unmade, and the slops not emptied. I looked in the wardrobe and the chest of drawers. Both were empty, so I realised, with a sense of panic, that once again we were without a maid.

I thought of having Norah back, baby and all. I was much too ahead of my time. Irish public opinion could not take it.

I have forgotten how many maids we had in five years – there must have been at least seven. I think they took advantage of my youth and inexperience, and for various reasons had difficulty in getting situations. Apart from the pregnant ones, three stand out. One said she had had her money stolen from under her bed. Desperate not to be without a maid, I did not tell my father. Instead I repaid her out of the first money I got for teaching. She turned out to be mentally disturbed, and eventually gave notice.

A most competent woman, a Protestant, answered the advertisement for a general. She was a wonderful cook, and for a few weeks we had marvellous food. She seemed too good to be true – and was! She turned out to be an alcoholic, and got so drunk she had to be dismissed. Sadly I saw her go, though I did not know at the time that the whiskey kept for visitors in the dining-room sideboard went with her!

I engaged what seemed to be a very suitable girl, country born with good references, and the slim figure I had learnt to look for. Her brother brought her one afternoon in a donkey cart. She had a large brown tin trunk which he humped up the stairs to her room for her.

I showed her round and then left her to unpack. About an hour later, I heard a curious noise. I went into the kitchen. There was the new maid humping her trunk down the stairs.

'Where ever are you going?'

'Home. I'll not stay here.'

'Why ever not?'

'It's haunted.'

'Haunted! Rubbish! Who ever told you that?'

'The gossoons. They told me that the ghost of Sir George walks every night.'

The gossoons were my young brothers. They got the rough side of my tongue. But the maid went.

This saga of the maids is not without its lighter side. I had one, another Mary, who was not too bright. I carefully supervised her a few times on how to cook a rolled rib of beef – our usual Sunday joint.

'Now Mary, weigh the joint.' She did that.

'How much does it weigh?'

'Seven pounds.'

'Good! And how long will you cook it?'

'Twenty minutes to the pound and twenty minutes over.' That had gone in.

'Yes, so you must cook it for two hours forty minutes. Put it in at ten and take it out at twenty minutes to one.'

'Yes, miss.'

She was able to read the clock.

One Sunday, I left her to cook the joint while we went to church. I hurried back ahead of the others. As I got to the door of the kitchen I smelt scorching meat and hurried in. There, on our biggest frying pan on top of the range, was the joint!

'Mary, what ever are you doing?'

'The oven wouldn't heat up, miss.'

I put my hand into the large oven. It was barely warm. I opened the little trap-door in the flue and pushed the flue poker in. It met the resistance of accumulated soot. 'Mary, you can't have cleaned out the flues on Friday! No wonder the oven's cold!'

'Oh, miss, I believe I forgot.'

With one exception, all the maids we had were devout Catholics. I was always interested in what Protestants called 'Catholic goings-on'.

'It's Ash Wednesday tomorrow, miss. Can I go for the ashes?' Maggie looked at me, hestitatingly.

'The ashes! What d'you mean?'

'The priest'll put ashes on me forehead. It's to remind me I'm mortal.'

'Yes, Maggie, of course you can go.'

'It'll be a black fast too.'

'Yes, I know that. What can you have?'

'Just a cup of black tea all day.'

'Nothing to eat?'

'Well, I'm allowed a bit of ling, but I don't like to bother you.'

'I'll get you a bit on my way back from school.'

I bought the ling, a large piece for tuppence. It was a yellowish-brown dried fish, very hard. It was also very salt.

'It makes you very thirsty,' Maggie told me. 'It's to remind you of our Lord's thirst on the Cross.'

'Do you only have it on Ash Wednesday?'

'We do, nowadays. Me grandma used to tell me it was used by very poor people instead of a herring, for "herring and point".'

'What ever's "herring and point"?'

'Well, if you're too poor to have a herring apiece, you get one herring and hang it up over potatoes. Then everyone points his potato at the herring. They say the potato gets the taste of the herring.'

A general maid's life in domestic service was not easy. Where there was only one maid it was lonely, especially if she came from the country parts. She was given her food from the family table. She took it into the kitchen to eat on her own. Our kitchen was at least light, airy and warm. She had a half-day free and an evening out, but she had to be in on the stroke of ten. On Sunday she went to early Mass. Wages were about twelve pounds a year for the untrained maid, living in, and all found. Aprons and caps were provided by the employer. In return, she was 'trained'.

I learnt much about domestic helps, and became increasingly tolerant. Each one had something to commend her. It was impossible to get all the domestic virtues in any one person. Who could expect it?

1920–22
Brother against brother

I was walking the mile home from Galway town. The reason I was walking and not cycling is clear from a letter I wrote in 1920: *I have given up riding the bicycle as the lorries go at about sixty miles an hour and skid all over the place. It was too much worry to keep out of their way.*

In the distance I heard the familiar sound. A lorry was approaching at breakneck speed. As the sound grew louder and louder, I crouched against the high walls of the Grammar School. Amid shouts of laughter, a hail of bullets flew over my head. The lorry was full of Black and Tans. They were in a cage of wire netting fastened to the sides of the lorry. Through this, they were pointing their rifles and firing indiscriminately as fancy took them. The lorry hurtled round the corner of the Oranmore Road and disappeared. One got used to anything!

I set off home.

Shall I put on my best blouse this evening? I wondered. I was asked out to tea at Mrs Semple's. She had left a note: *Can you come to tea at six this evening and help me entertain an unexpected guest? No need to reply: just turn up.*

Promptly at six o'clock, I rang Mrs Semple's bell.

She opened the door. 'Good. I'm glad you've managed it. Give me your things.' She took my hat and coat and hung them on a coatstand made of a deer's antlers.

'Now, come and meet Duncan. I met him at church on Sunday. He seemed lonely, so I asked him along.' She opened the drawing-room door. A young man stood up. To my amazement, he wore the uniform of the Black and Tans – a khaki tunic and black trousers. The wearers got their nickname from a famous black-and-tan pack of hounds in County Cork.

'How d'ye do?' The voice was unmistakably Scottish.

The door opened. A maid came in. 'Tea's ready, ma'am.'

'Thank you, Rosie.'

In the dining-room, we did full justice to Mrs Semple's high tea of cold chicken and ham, fresh scones and plum cake. The conversation was very general – the nice weather we were having: the hope that it would hold for the Flower Show. I felt very uneasy. I was sitting at a meal with a Black and Tan opposite me. I began to feel again the early fear of the afternoon, and glanced at him. He had the typical hair of the Scot: sandy, tinged with red. His blue eyes were clear and honest-looking. But the uneasiness did not go.

After tea, we sat round the blazing log fire. 'Duncan's only been here for ten days. He's feeling very lonely.'

'Lonely!' Duncan sat up straight. 'Loneliness doesn't matter. It's that I'm just horrified.'

'Horrified?'

'Yes, I'd no idea what I was letting myself in for when I joined the Black and Tans.'

'Why did you?'

'I couldn't get a job after the war. I saw an advert asking for recruits to an auxiliary forces to help the police over here keep law and order. It seemed a worthwhile job.'

'Isn't it?'

'It could be. But most of my comrades seem to think they're a law unto themselves.'

I looked at him. 'Indeed, that's right,' I said. 'I was terrified this afternoon. I might have been killed if one of the bullets they were firing had gone astray.'

'That's just what I mean. I don't think they'd deliberately hurt a civilian, but they're trigger-happy. They think it's fun.'

'There's a rumour they've vandalised the library at the Lodge.'

'Has that got out? It's hard to believe. We're billeted in a lovely old house, but most of them have no respect for property. Only last night, I saw one tear a page from a leatherbound book – just to light a cigarette. I did try to stop him, but all I got was "Mind your own bloody business".'

Mrs Semple looked at Duncan. 'It's even worse than we thought. Can't you get out?'

'Some of us wish we could, but there isn't a hope.'

He put his head in his hands. I felt very embarrassed, and got up. 'I think I must go. I've still quite a lot of work to do for college tomorrow.' Mrs Semple nodded. She fetched my hat and coat. I turned to Duncan, but he did not look up.

As I walked home, my mind was confused. It was hard to connect the madmen in the lorry with the disillusioned young man in Mrs Semple's drawing-room.

'All right,' said the Professor of Mathematics, one Monday morning in November, 1920. 'I'll work out this problem for you, as it seems to be causing difficulty.'

As he turned to the blackboard the door flew open. About ten of the British armed forces burst into the lecture-room. They were men of the Sixth Dragoon Guards, then stationed in Galway. The professor went pale. He was known to have Sinn Fein sympathies. There was dead silence in the lecture-room. One sensed the feeling of fear. I felt a sort of coldness all over.

'Women out,' shouted the officer, 'the men line up.' There were three women, including myself. We gathered up our books and left the lecture-room. We had to pass through the college quadrangle. There we found about seventy of the men students lined up in rows. They were surrounded by soldiers with rifles and bayonets. Women students were huddled on the steps of the lecture-rooms. The Dragoon Guards' band was in one corner of the quadrangle.

When all the men, including the professors, had been put in ranks, the officer brought out a large Union Jack.

'It was some of you lot who kicked up a row last week,' he yelled. 'Now you're going to make up for it.' This row is mentioned in a letter I wrote:

> The last week had been very full and eventful. Of course the people did not want to keep Armistice Day here, but the Black and Tans posted up notices in every shop forbidding owners to open on pain of death. Every shop remained closed. Then at 11.00 am everybody in the street was made to stand still for two minutes. It is alleged that some of the College students kicked up a row.

The notice was typewritten. It was quoted in the *Connaught Tribune*:

> You are ordered to keep your premises shut all day on 11 November in memory of the gallant lads who fell for the sake of old England and the R.I.C. who were murdered by their own countrymen. Any person who disobeys this order will have no roof over their heads in twenty-four hours.
> Penalty 308 Mills No. 5
> BEWARE!

In the quadrangle, the Union Jack was unfurled. The band struck up *God save the King*. Many of the women students sat down and sang *The Soldiers' Song*. They yelled against the playing of the National Anthem: 'Soldiers are we whose lives are pledged to Ireland.'

I was standing with my sister and another Protestant student. There was only a handful of Protestants in the College. What should we do? The National Anthem was being played. From childhood, we had been taught to stand at attention. I saw my companion was standing stiffly at attention and singing, 'Send him victorious, happy and glorious.' I did nothing – just stood there.

It was all over in a matter of minutes. Three men students who refused to remove their caps were arrested and marched into one of the lecture-rooms. One student, asked why he had refused to remove his cap, is alleged to have said, 'in protest against recent murders'.

'Murders! What murders? Just name one.'

'Mrs Quinn.'

Mrs Quinn was a young pregnant mother. She was sitting on a wall outside her village home, a child in her arms. A lorry load of Black and Tans drove wildly through the village. Mrs Quinn was hit by a bullet and died soon after. None but the witnesses were allowed into the court for the investigation of the incident.

Of the incident in the College quadrangle, I wrote in the same letter: *We all agreed that the whole proceeding was rather silly.* Silly or not, I felt as I walked home that the British had let us down.

However, the incident was indeed 'silly' compared with other events of that November in 1920.

Late on a Saturday afternoon, I was in a hurry to get home. Suddenly, I became aware that nearly everyone had a local newspaper. I stopped by three women huddled behind a wide-open paper.

'Has something happened?'

'Indade yes, Father Griffin's been found murdered.' She showed me the paper, its columns outlined in black.

'Shure it's the grand priest he was – a good word for everyone. I bet it's them murdering Black and Tans. England's a lot to answer for.'

Used as I was to almost daily acts of violence, I felt a deep sense of shock. Even to me, a Protestant, the killing of a priest seemed a particular outrage.

Before I could say anything, the woman went on: 'It says here that about half-past twelve three men called for him. They pretended it was a sick call. Father Griffin went out with them. No one set eyes on him since.'

'Where's he been found?'

'In Barna Woods – two bullets through his head.'

Barna Woods, I thought – where we used to play as children. It seemed to increase the sense of shock.

Father Griffin was a popular priest. Whatever his political views may have been, his opposition to violence was well known. 'Let none of you touch a policeman,' he said again and again, in sermons and elsewhere. 'He's there to do his duty, to keep Law and Order.' His murderers were never identified.

His funeral was remarkable.

The headline in the *Connaught Tribune* was: *'Father Griffin Goes Home. Universal Representation. 1500 Uncovered Heads.'*

The report said:

> In the vast crowd that awaited the funeral, every section of life in the city and surrounding districts was represented: the Protestant Rector, his curate, and practically every member of his congregation, Presbyterians and Methodists, leading landowners, and their humblest tenants and servants.

A faded old photograph shows this vast crowd. The hearse, drawn by the traditional black-plumed horses, is hard to distinguish from the people lining the streets from wall to wall. The driver of the hearse stands out, because of his top hat with flowing mourning drapes. In the next week, he, too, was shot.

Father Griffin must indeed have been 'a good man', who could unite in his death those who viewed each other with prejudice, suspicion and fear.

'Did you ever know a guerilla war that failed?' asked my brother Alec a few years ago. 'Think of Ireland in 1921.'

What he said was indeed true, for in 1921 the IRA had retreated to the mountains. From there, with considerable public support, they carried on a guerilla war on which martial law and reprisals by the British side had little effect.

In the same year, the British prime minister, Lloyd George, suggested a cease-fire. Perhaps surprisingly, it was accepted by de Valera, the IRA leader, and negotiations were begun. Events moved rapidly, and on 6 December 1921, a treaty was signed by which Ireland was to be partitioned. Part of Ulster, the six counties, was to have its own parliament. The other six counties accepted dominion status, and became the Free State of Eire.

We heard the news at breakfast time the next day, as usual from the *Irish Times*.

'This is the biggest mistake the British have ever made,' remarked my father. 'It's going to mean endless trouble.' He little knew how prophetically he spoke.

A short time later, he came into the kitchen where Tom, his general man, was separating the milk. 'Well, Tom,' he asked, 'how do you like our new government?'

'I'm agin' it sor,' replied Tom.

Tom was not the only one to be against the Free State. There were those who felt that their leaders had sold out to the British, and the immediate result of the Treaty was a split in Sinn Fein. The majority, including most Protestants, accepted the new government led by Arthur Griffith and Michael Collins. The opposition, led by de Valera, formed itself, in effect, into an army, and began a campaign against the Free State. It was no longer the Irish nationalists against the British: it was brother against brother.

'The whole world's in a state of chassis.' This remark of 'Captain' Jack Boyle in Sean O'Casey's play *Juno and the Paycock* sums up the situation. For over a year there was civil war, and life was lived in a state of uncertainty. Never a day passed without word of some incident. Some were comparatively trivial: some were even funny, but many more brought death and destruction to innocent civilians. Perhaps the saddest thing was the divided loyalties in so many Irish homes.

One morning I was on my way into Galway. I stopped to have a word with Mrs O'Flanagan, a widow, who was leaning over the half-door of her cottage. 'And how are you these days, Mrs O'Flanagan?'

'Not so good, not so good – you see it's me lads.'

'Your lads?'

'Yes, me lads. Patrick has joined up in the Free State army – it's a grand sight he is in his green uniform – and of course, he's already a good hand with a gun. It's like he'll be made a corporal.'

'Well now, isn't that good news – so what's the trouble?'

'It's this way. The other lad, Gerald, says Collins is a traitor, so he's gone off to join the Irregulars – to free Ireland, he says. What in the name of God do they think they've been doing all these years? Wouldn't you think he'd be satisfied with his father kilt in an ambush – God rest his soul.' She crossed herself.

'Where's Gerald now?'

'On the run somewhere. I haven't seen him for weeks. He daren't show up at home in case Patrick was on leave – it's brother against brother now.'

'I'm so sorry. It must make you very anxious.'

'It's hardly a wink of sleep I get. I keep thinking I hear footsteps coming to the door. Every time there's a knock, I put up a prayer, "Holy Mother of God, don't let it be my baby Gerald". I open the door expecting to see Gerald's body on a gate. As often as not it's Mrs Walsh wanting to borrow a pinch o' tay. She's a one, I can tell you.'

'Well, I hope that whenever you open the door to a knock, it'll be no one worse than Mrs Walsh! I must be off. Goodbye now for the present.'

'Goodbye. God be with you, miss.'

I had been away for a few days visiting my grandfather. My father met me at the station. He took my little suitcase.

'All right to walk?' he asked. 'I'm still afraid the Irregulars will commandeer the car, if I take it out.' We started to walk the mile home.

'How's your grandpa?'

'He's really very well. He's grumbling about his new dentures. I don't think the dentist can do much more for him.'

We walked in silence for some minutes. Then my father turned to me.

'Do you have the key of your desk?'

'Yes, it's in my handbag. I locked the desk before I left. Why?' I looked at him questioningly.

'Well, I'm afraid we had a visit from the Irregulars last night.'

'Goodness, what happened?'

'I was awakened by the sound of voices. It must have been about half-past one. I got the lamp lit and found Alec in the hall, surrounded by six Irregulars. He had let them in.'

'Did you know any of them?'

'No. They were the usual lot. More or less in their uniform – fawn macks, mufflers. Two had black Homburg hats. The others had those tweed caps worn at an angle. Each had a gun of some sort. "Now, Sor, this is a raid. We've had word you've guns and ammunition," the leader said, when I came down the stairs. "Commandant's orders."

' "I haven't a gun in the house," I told them. "Police orders: I took them all to the police station." Suddenly, one of them took me by the arm, seized the lamp and pinned me against the wall.

Another pointed a gun at me.

' "What do you think of the Lord Mayor of Cork?" he asked.

' "If he doesn't give up his fast soon, he'll die."

' "Bet you don't care."

' "Of course I care! I'm sorry when any man dies unnecessarily." Fortunately they dropped the matter of McSweeney. Two of them kept me pinned to the wall. Two others rushed upstairs to your room. Ella had not wakened. "Ask them not to disturb the child," I called. "She'll be dreadfully frightened." One man went up. Then all three came down. One held the old air rifle.

' "Thought you said all the guns were with the polis."

' "I'd forgotten that airgun. The boys keep it to shoot at crows."

' "There's a locked desk in the room. Where's the key now?"

' "It's my daughter's. She's away. If it's locked, she must have the key with her."

' "What's in it?"

' "I've no idea." The leader looked at one of the men. "G'on up, Kevin, and see what's in it. Maybe that's where the ammunition's hidden. Mind the child now."

'Kevin went up the stairs, two shallow steps at a time. He was back in a few minutes. "Nothing in it but letters and the like." '

My father and I walked in silence for a few minutes. The oak desk was my pride and joy, the family present on my recent twenty-first birthday, the first bit of furniture I'd ever owned. I ventured the question now uppermost in my mind: 'Is the desk badly damaged?'

'I'm afraid it's rather messed up, but I think we can get it mended.'

I felt sorry I'd been away. We took raids and shootings for granted. I'd missed all the excitement. If I'd been at home, they wouldn't have broken the desk.

'Did the Irregulars go then?'

'Not they! "Now, Sor, we've word there's ammunition in the house," said the leader chap.

' "Well, find it," I said.'

'Have you any?' I asked.

'Only about fifty cartridges the police let me keep for my work. They'll bring out my gun if I need it. I must be able to destroy an animal. You know there's no other way.'

I knew that was true. More than once I'd seen an old decrepit donkey, starved, full of sores and beyond any vet's help, led out into the field by Tom. Over its head he put a sack. The donkey was placed on the edge of a pit, dug to receive it. With one shot from my father's gun, invariably accurate, the animal was put out of its misery. Much as I hated it, I knew there was no other way.

My father continued: 'What do you think they meant by "We've had word"?'

'Might be bluff.'

'I sometimes wonder if Delia doesn't chat to that follower of hers.'

'I don't know. Could be. I'll keep my ears open. But go on. What happened next?' I asked.

' "We'll do a real search of the house, me boys," said the leader. With that he gave me back the lamp. He had the oldest pistol I'd ever seen in my life. I doubt if it could be fired, but one never knows. He stuck the pistol in my back and marched me round the house looking for this ammunition. In the surgery, they found my Sam Browne belt and my leggings.

' "They'll be no use to you. They're British," I reminded them. They made no reply, just took them. We came last to the dining-room. One chap pulled open the sideboard cupboard. There were only about two tots of whiskey in the decanter. Each one took a swig. Suddenly, they looked at the bookcase. I'd put the box of cartridges on the top of some books. It was to keep it out of the way of the children.

' "What's in that cupboard?"

' "Well, you can see, books."

'I held the lamp, so that the leaden lights of the doors reflected the light downwards. To my relief, they did not open the doors. The leader then put the men in military formation. "Quick march," he said. Off they went down the hall and out of the side door.'

'Did Ella wake up?' I asked.

'No, she slept through it all. We haven't told her. Best not. You know, we got off very lightly, when you think of what some have had!'

Some weeks later, a meal was ready waiting for my father's return. A car, a somewhat battered Ford, drew into the backyard. My father got out accompanied by two men. Each wore a belted trench coat and black Homburg hat. To my surprise, they followed him into the kitchen. This was odd. People wanting my father usually waited on chairs by the side door.

'I've got to go on a milk fever case,' he said. 'These gentlemen are looking after me.'

'What about your dinner?'

'I won't wait.'

He went into the surgery to collect the milk fever apparatus. It included a large syringe. The two men followed him, and I began to feel uneasy. Were the men following him deliberately? Was it just curiosity to see what was in the surgery? All three came out of the surgery, one carrying the syringe. They went down the long passage to the dining-room.

'Would you bring a jug of water?' my father called. Delia was on holiday, so I took a jug of water. Each man had a whiskey. This was odder still. The men were not the kind usually entertained in the dining-room.

'Will you be back before the curfew?' My father did not reply. All three went out by the side door. I heard the car drive off. I was alone in the house as the children had gone to England. I felt quite frightened. Had my father really gone on a case? Curfew time came. There was no sign of my father's return.

Tom came in from his cottage just across the road. 'Shall I go for the polis, miss?' he asked.

'It'ud be no use. There's not a thing they could do. Anyway, it's better not to break the curfew.'

'Shall I stay with you?'

'No thanks, Tom. I'll be all right. You get off to bed.'

I put up the shutters in all the downstairs rooms. I locked all doors, something we seldom did. Then I tried to concentrate on writing an essay. The quietness seemed uncanny. Not once did I hear a car or a horse pass in the road. About half-past ten, I thought I heard a car. I listened. The drive gate clicked shut. I heard my father's footsteps on the gravel, but waited for him to knock on the door. We had learnt to be very cautious. My father came in. He looked tired out.

'Where ever have you been all this time?'

'Some farm in Connemara. I thought I knew the country well, but I've never been to that farm.'

'Where was it?'

'I don't know. When we got a few miles out, they blindfolded me. We got to a farm, about twenty-five miles away, I judge. I found a valuable cow in a bad state. She'll recover. They brought me into the farm and gave me a good meal. They've paid my fee. Hardly a word was spoken, except about the cow.'

'Was coming home easier?'

'Yes, they did not blindfold me as it was dark. We twisted and turned in the lanes. We only hit the main road about two miles up.'

'Who do you think they are?'

'Irregulars, I'm pretty sure. The farm kitchen didn't give anything away: just the usual Catholic stuff – no thanks, I don't want anything to eat. I'll just get off to bed.'

With a great sense of relief, I went round putting out the lamps.

On another occasion I was again alone in the house, except for Delia. She was in the kitchen, a flight of stairs, a long passage, and two swing doors away. There was a loud knocking on the front door. I expected to see a farmer wanting my father. Instead, I saw two youths of about seventeen. Each wore a shabby green tunic much too big for him. The sleeves of the smaller lad were turned up about six inches, the dirty brown lining making a kind of cuff. The tunics were belted with webbing. The trousers of the smaller lad fitted him quite well: the bigger boy had his pin-striped trousers tied up with string just above the ankles. The tweed caps at an angle told me that two Irregulars were calling on me. I felt slightly uneasy, but decided they looked pretty harmless.

'My father's not in,' I began.

'We don't want the vet. The Commandant's sent us to collect the Boy Scout uniforms. We know you have them.'

My uneasiness increased. How did they know about the uniforms? They hadn't been worn for two or three years.

My brothers had been Boy Scouts before the troubles began. I'd seen the uniforms in a cupboard in their room only a few days ago.

I looked at the odd pair standing on the doorstep. They didn't seem to be armed. There were no pockets in the tunics. I decided to try some bluff.

'You're collecting uniforms for the Irregulars, are you?'

'Yes, miss.'

'But they're khaki! You won't want khaki, surely?'

'My mother can dye them.' The smaller one was the leader.

'All right then,' I said to him. 'Show me your search warrant.' One looked at the other.

'Warrant. Sure we haven't got no warrant.'

'Well, go back to your Commandant and get a warrant. When you bring it back, I'll let you look for the uniforms. I doubt though you'll find any.'

The bluff worked. The two lads set off, not down the drive, but across the fields. So that was how they'd managed to get to the house unobserved.

I rushed upstairs to the boys' room. I opened the large mahogany cupboard. Yes, there were two shelves full of Boy Scout uniforms. There were two khaki shirts, the sleeves covered in badges, Birdwatcher, Electrician, Cook, Historian among them. Working for those badges had kept the boys out of mischief! There were two pairs of khaki shorts, two broad-brimmed scout hats and four green scarves. As well, there was a miscellaneous collection of equipment, whistles, lanyards, a jack-knife, and neatly folded up, a small Union Jack. I decided to leave them.

I gathered up all the uniforms, found an old sheet in the linen cupboard and tied them up in a big bundle. I took the bundle out by the side door, and round the house to the stables. I wanted to avoid the kitchen window. Delia was fairly new. I wasn't sure about her politics. Did she know about the uniforms? She could easily have seen them, as the cupboard was not locked. Had she told the Irregulars about them? One could never know. Again, it might be brother against brother.

In the stables, I found an empty grain sack and stuffed the uniforms inside. Just to be sure, I left it and looked into the kitchen: 'Everything all right, Delia?'

'Yes, miss, I'm just going to set the table.'

Delia took the large black enamel tray of cutlery and set it down on the long dresser. She pushed through the swing doors with her shoulder, and set off down the long passage to the dining-room.

I hurried back to the stables, opened the wooden-barred gate, and dragged the sack, heavier than I had expected, across to the cesspool in the field beyond. All household waste accumulated in this big cesspool which was cleared out every few months.

Would I be able to lift the cover? That was my worry as I crossed the field. I just managed to push the heavy wooden cover about a foot back. I dropped in the shirts. They floated on the grey sticky mess. I found a stick in the field and pushed the shirts under with the stick. Then in turn, in went shorts, hats, scarves. I watched each garment gradually absorb the smelly liquid as I held it down. Try as I would, I couldn't push the cover back. It was too heavy. I had to leave it.

When I got back to the house, I found that my father had just come in.

'Could you put the cover back on the cesspool, please?'

'The cesspool! How in the world's the cover got off the cesspool.'

I told him the story. He laughed.

'I don't think they'll come back. They'll be afraid we'll give a description to the Free State soldiers.'

My father was right. We did not see those lads again.

1919–22
'The Idea of a University'

'Don't be frightened, Mr Burglar. I don't want to hurt you.'

I heard the words behind me as I walked across the quadrangle on my first day at the university. I turned and looked at the speaker. He was a tall man in his middle twenties. He was smiling at me. Then I knew who it was – Robin Wallis.

About seven years before, his father, the Methodist minister, had come into the Model School. 'Have you a girl here who could learn up a part in a sketch overnight?' he asked. 'The girl who was to do it has got measles.'

Mr Brown looked at me. 'Yes, I have, but I'm not sure if her mother will agree.'

I was called out. The situation was explained to me. One thing I could do was to learn by heart very quickly. I too was not sure about mother, though. She had the Scottish Puritan's fear that acting might be of the Devil!

'I'll cycle out and see her,' said Mr Wallis. In about an hour, he was back.

'It's quite all right. I've settled with your mother that you may come to the Manse for a rehearsal after school. We'll give you something to eat.'

Two evenings later, dressed in a cream flannelette nightdress, my hair floating round my shoulders, and to my mother's horror, holding a naked lighted candle, I made my début as an actress. I was interrupting a burglar, acted by Robin, already a young man. My first words were to reassure him that as a burglar, he had nothing to fear from me! They were the words with which he greeted me when, unexpectedly, we met again so many years later.

Robin was one of many young men whose university education was interrupted by the First World War. He survived, and with several older students was drafted by the government to Galway, where there was plenty of room. The medical and engineering schools had a very good reputation. These older students, with their wartime experiences, brought an unusual stability and maturity to the first-year undergraduates that year.

University College, Galway, was one of the so-called 'godless colleges' in Ireland. Technically, they were non-denominational. No chair of theology was allowed in them. Hence the name.

Established in 1845, the Queen's Colleges, the first state-built university in Britain, were an attempt to meet the demand for a Catholic system of education in Ireland. Before 1845, Trinity College, Dublin, a Tudor foundation, was the only university in Ireland. It was the stronghold of the Protestant ascendancy. Catholics were allowed to take degrees there from 1793, but were debarred from scholarships or Fellowships.

The Catholic hierarchy was given a major role on the governing bodies of the Queen's Colleges. Because of their 'godless' nature they did not meet with favour among Catholics. In fact, Catholics were discouraged from attending them. It was not until 1908 that the Queen's Colleges of Dublin, Cork and Galway became the National University of Ireland. Galway, in particular, became the seat of the revival of the Irish language.

In my day, Galway was a small intimate college of probably not more than three hundred students. The teaching staff was highly qualified. Both in work and behaviour, an equally high standard was demanded of students. Cardinal Newman's *Idea of a University*, written when he was Rector of the Dublin College, was required reading for every student.

It is with gratitude that I recognise the sound academic background for teaching that I got in Galway. The college, however, was limited in what it allowed of the wider aspects of university life.

Liberal as was Cardinal Newman's idea of a Catholic university, he was certain that, *a university cannot exist externally to the Catholic pale . . . Hence, a direct and active jurisdiction of the Church over it and in it, is necessary, lest it should become the rival of the Church.*

As a woman student, I was very conscious of the restrictions, often trivial, imposed because of the moral jurisdiction of the Church. To take one example, the personal appearance and social life of the women students were strictly supervised. I was soon to find this out.

'The Lady Superintendent wants to see you immediately,' called Maria Flynn, as she hurtled across the quad to a lecture. 'Can't stop. I'm late already.'

Lateness for a lecture was a cardinal sin.

I was surprised. Wants to see me! What ever for? I was not aware of having broken any rules. I felt a sudden fear. Was something wrong with one of the children? I too hurried across the quad, then I knocked on the Lady Superintendent's office door.

'Come in.' I went in. She was busy writing and did not look up. She did not ask me to sit down. Her hair piled neatly on her head, her navy-blue dress, white linen collar and cuffs seemed to give a sense of cold efficiency. For another minute she went on with her writing. Then she blotted it and covered it with the blotting paper. Did she think I was trying to read what she had written? Nothing was further from my mind. I felt very long and thin as I stood towering over the desk.

Suddenly she looked up, glaring at me and said: 'That hair won't do: you'll have to put it up properly!'

'That hair' was currently the bane of my existence. It was waist length, fine and very unruly. All my attempts to get it to stay up in a bun had failed.

'Well,' I stuttered, 'well – I put the bow on to help keep my hair up.' I had tied a piece of black ribbon at the end of a long plait and rolled the plait up to the back of my head. It seemed the solution. The hairpins did not fall out every time I moved.

'Ribbons are not allowed in College. You should know that. See that you have your hair up properly tomorrow.' She returned to her writing.

Next day, I turned up at the President's lecture in Experimental Physics. My hair was coiled in a bun at the back of my head. It was secured by almost a whole packet of hairpins, bought at Moon's shop on my way home. I was aware of the hairpins sticking into my scalp. Every now and then one fell out. I hoped the bun would stay up for the length of the lecture.

There were comparatively few women in the university. A science subject or logic was compulsory for all first-year students, and most women opted for logic. About four of us attended the physics lectures. The women sat on the front row of the gallery lecture-room. Behind us rose tier on tier of men, engineering and medical students.

The President came in. All chattering stopped immediately and the students stood. The President mounted the dais. He was short and rotund, dressed in a cutaway morning coat and dark trousers. A voluminous aged gown trailed down his back. He was a most distinguished scientist, though his ability was not generally recognised.

'Be kind enough to turn out the light.' The President looked at a student near the light switch.

'Certainly, sir.' The light went out. The lecture was, in fact, part of a series on light. The President turned to a slide reflected on a screen from a sophisticated magic lantern. The slide showed a human eye. It was most interesting.

'When an image falls short of the retina . . .' The President pointed with his long black stick.

But I did not then hear what happened to that image. I felt a movement behind me. Something touched me; suddenly my hair cascaded round my shoulders. A student behind me had inserted a ruler into the bun. There was a suspicion of giggles.

The President stopped. 'If any gentleman is not interested in this lecture, he has my permission to leave the lecture-room.'

There was silence immediately. Discipline in a lecture-room was as strict as it had been in school. Hairpins were everywhere. I managed to grasp the long mane of hair and plait it.

'Please, let me get it up before the light goes on,' I murmured. The darkness helped. Surreptitiously, I retrieved a few hairpins, and secured the plait on top of my head. I knew that the only way to avoid such disasters was to have my hair bobbed.

Bobbed hair was just coming into fashion, but in the West of Ireland it was still considered a sign of wildness. My father agreed, and, for me, one problem at the university was solved.

Since I lived at home, the Lady Superintendent had no jurisdiction over me outside the college. She did, however, keep a stern eye on the women students in lodgings, where most of them lived.

A woman student shall not be out after 10.00 pm read one of the regulations. It is interesting to note in this day of equality of the sexes, that the licence to be out was extended to 11.00 pm for men students!

It was partly due to the strict discipline, both at home and in the college, that I was able to keep up with my studies. I did not choose the easiest of optional first-year subjects. Experimental physics and mathematics involved really hard paper work. But I am glad I made that choice. They were the only glimpse into scientific knowledge I ever had. What I learnt in the physics lectures has often proved of much practical value. It is interesting to know the difference between short sight and long sight and what is meant by astigmatism. Insights into the nature of electricity have again and again had practical uses. One lecture described a Leclanché cell. As I looked at this oblong glass container, I realised that the long row of such containers on a shelf in our kitchen, were indeed Leclanché cells. Each was connected to a bell, but none of the bells had ever worked in my memory. I got some sal ammoniac, made a solution and filled the container connected to the front doorbell. What a thrill of achievement, and indeed of amazement, I felt when the front doorbell rang.

The mathematics was of the old-fashioned kind: Euclid, trigonometry, differential and integral calculus. Without it, I should never have got a teaching post in the 1930s. It was then, as now, a shortage subject, especially in girls' schools. To reach the required standard was largely a matter of application in ploughing through the exercises in the textbooks.

So long as my younger sister was at home, we managed the housekeeping between us quite easily. When she went to college in England, things became more difficult. Much depended on the efficiency of the current maid.

I think I inherited a portion of a family gift for organisation. The adequate feeding of the whole family was the priority. I made out a menu for a fortnight, so that shepherd's pie was not always on Tuesday and Irish stew on Thursday. Friday was easy. No one thought of having anything but fish on that day! Herrings were two for three halfpence. Roast beef, Yorkshire pudding and a fruit pie were the invariable Sunday lunch. A fairly efficient maid, given some training, coped with the day-to-day cooking. Shopping was easy. A list of requirements in a special book was handed in to the grocer and the butcher every week. Every shop delivered goods. Milk, vegetables and fruit were home-grown.

Saturday morning was set aside for other cooking, which fortunately I liked doing. I made a batch of soda bread, white and brown. Sometimes, I added a treacle or a carraway loaf. Most households ate home-made soda bread. Baker's bread was a treat. A batch of scones followed and, generally, a big flat apple tart for my elder brother, who was a weekly boarder in the Grammar School.

Alternate weeks, I made a large sponge cake, five eggs beaten by hand for twenty minutes with caster sugar, and then flour folded in. This was a great favourite with visitors, especially if some cream was spared from the butter-making. On the alternate week, I made a plum cake, my father's favourite.

Mother used to churn the cream from the milk of our two

cows. The churn was a small barrel type, worked by hand. When, after my mother's death, I had to learn Irish, I often propped the Irish grammar on the churn and chanted the vocabulary to the rhythm of the splashing milk. When the rhythm altered, it meant the milk was breaking. What a relief to lift up the lid and see the golden granules of butter. That was the moment to stop turning the handle. Mother had always done the churning, and I'd watched often enough. The first time I did it myself all went well until the butter formed. Then I was absolutely flummoxed. How did one get the butter out of the churn? Instinctively, I thought, 'I'll go and ask mother.' Then, for the first time, it came upon me forcibly that she was no longer there.

The routine for homework established by mother continued. Immediately after six-o'clock tea, we all settled down to our respective bits of preparation. I looked forward to two or three hours' study. There were, of course, the occasional interruptions, if a brother or sister needed help. I always had the head of the table. My younger brother Alec often had trouble over maths.

'Fran,' Alec looked at me, 'Mr Hannington said I was to get you to give me a hand with this algebra. I could not make out what he was talking about.'

Evening after evening this happened. Alec, because of his height, one suspected, had been moved up a form ahead of his age group. There were great gaps in his knowledge as a result. Sometimes I resented the time it took to explain the problem. After all, a teacher was paid to teach. But the time I gave, usually willingly, brought an unexpected bonus. It proved to be of great value when I became a teacher, especially in the teaching of maths.

There were no modern temptations such as television or radio. As the younger ones finished, they played games, Happy Families or Snap, or went on with a hobby. The boys had good collections of birds' eggs and of cigarette cards. We were all usually in bed by half-past nine.

As the pressure of college work increased, there was need for more study. I have never needed a great deal of sleep. I am also much better at learning in the early morning. So I took a bowl of cold water up to my room, set the alarm clock for five o'clock, and when it went off, douched my face with cold water. Then, wide awake, I was able to do two hours of study before getting up.

There was no gas or electricity in the house. Sometimes, if it were very cold, I lit the paraffin stove. A candle on the bedside table was all the light there was. Usually, I put on a warm dressing jacket. I seldom attempted written work. English was my main subject, so there was endless reading to be done. Propped up by two feather pillows, with the bedclothes humped up to make a bookrest, morning after morning, I read my way through the set books. There were plays of Marlowe and Shakespeare, part of Spenser's *Faerie Queene*, the Metaphysical poets, Steele, Swift and so on, through selections of eighteenth- and nineteenth-century literature. I noted down appropriate quotations that might be useful in answering an examination question.

According to Presbyterian custom, no study was allowed on Sunday. I often think that day, free from the pressures of the week, was indeed my salvation.

Life was not all hard work. We were fortunate in having a tennis court. We children cut it, rolled it and marked it. Most days in the summer we had some games of tennis. As soon as I was seventeen, I was allowed to take a rowing boat up the River Corrib. This we often did on fine Saturday afternoons in the summer.

I loved the river. The rhythm of rowing – inserting the oar blades into the water, so that there was no splash, then turning them sharply to skim the water with the gentlest of feathers – was a wonderful relaxation after a hard morning's mental work.

We never rowed if the water was rough. We had all learnt the rules of the river. We knew, for instance, how to change places with safety. Nevertheless, I always felt it a responsibility when I had the younger ones with me. Sometimes it was hard to prevent a certain amount of larking about. By this time, we could all swim, but never thought of taking life-saving jackets with us, as I find is the custom today.

Very often we were alone in the house. My father was kept very busy. He was the only veterinary surgeon for miles around. It was not unusual for him to have an urgent call at night. If he were free, he often went to join other men in a club in town. Fifty years later, a school friend said to me: 'That club brought unhappiness to all our mothers.'

There was little else for men to do. But the treating to rounds of drinks meant that money was spent that should have gone towards the family upkeep. I was not the only daughter who dreaded the return of a father from the club, and wondered what sort of mood he would be in. One has to recognise that, for my father, a widower with the responsibility of five children, life cannot have been easy.

On Sunday, and such days as he was not in town, my father was full of fun. 'Who'd like the first cut?' he asked every now and then, as he cut the apple pie. Always slow in the uptake, I was caught out, amid roars of laughter from the others. It was only years later that I saw the point. *Two* cuts are needed to make a slice.

Once a week, if he were in, my father took us to the pictures. He always had complimentary tickets, given instead of a fee. I did not always go, unless Charlie Chaplin were on the programme. We all loved him, with his little moustache, tiny hat and large feet. I hated films that showed violence or bloodshed. The films were, of course, in black and white and silent, so I could shut my eyes to avoid seeing anything I did not want to see. A piano provided background music.

Education had high priority in Irish families, whether Protestant or Catholic. Secondary education was not free. Catholic families sacrificed much to educate a priest or a nun, for to have one in the family was a great honour.

Protestants, on the whole, had better educational facilities. For one thing, there were fewer of them, and some schools and colleges had good endowments. My brothers were able to become weekly boarders because of scholarships awarded only to Protestants.

Unless a student were fortunate enough to win one of the few open scholarships to the university, all fees had to be found. I did not win a scholarship for my first year. I supplemented what my family could afford by doing some teaching. I had a beginner's Latin class for those who needed this compulsory subject for Matriculation and charged sixpence an hour. If I had a group of five, I got half-a-crown, quite an amount of money in those days!

A letter to my aunt written in December, 1920, shows that I was doing some teaching in the High School: *I got £10 for teaching in school last term. I had 80 hours altogether. It will be very useful just now, as I have nearly £5 worth of books to get – mainly English ones. I think they will be useful later on.*

Yes, life was very full, but I was highly motivated to get knowledge. I was not terribly ambitious and was content to pass my exams reasonably well. On the occasions I did very well, I always felt guilty. Why, I never discovered.

'There's not a scrap of romance in you,' said Elizabeth. I forget what prompted this remark. I think she was right. I was so busy with home and college that, consciously or unconsciously, I shut out the idea of romance. Anyway, I was plain. I certainly thought that to have a romance, one had to be good-looking. I read, however, a great deal of romantic poetry and classic fiction, and identified myself with the heroines. Probably fantasy was the substitute for reality.

For the first time, I had access to a library – the university was well-stocked with a wide diversity of books.

'May I have this book, please?'

The librarian, also Professor of the few philosophy students, looked at it. 'I'd much rather you didn't read this book – at least until you're older.'

The book was one on psychic phenomena by Oliver Lodge. It was about his son, Raymond, killed in the war.

'I won't be influenced by it. I think I'm old enough to make up my own mind.'

'How old are you?'

'Nineteen.'

'Young, very young. You don't know what harm a book like this could do to you. I can't refuse to let you have it, but it would please me very much if you promised not to read this book for the present.'

Once again, I became aware of the indirect influence of the Catholic Church. I hadn't the courage to refuse him, but however kindly meant, I resented the implied restriction of my intellectual freedom.

There was one place where speech was neither censored nor restricted – the Literary and Debating Society. The curfew meant that I was not able to take part in many of the university activities since we lived about two miles away. I tried to get to every meeting, though I never dared to speak.

One evening, at the close of the meeting, the chairman looked at me. 'It's time you opened your mouth,' he said. 'I'm putting you down to propose the motion next time.'

He gave me no chance to refuse, and proceeded to read out the subject for the next debate: 'The downfall of Napoleon was due to his overweening ambition.'

I was literally struck dumb. What a subject! Panic-stricken, I rushed up to him. He was gathering up his papers. The room was emptying fast: people wanted to get home. The caretaker stood at the door, keys in hand.

'I can't – I don't want – I don't know anything about Napoleon.'

The chairman cut me short. 'Oh, yes you do. It was the period for the Senior Grade. You'll do fine. So long.' He disappeared through the door.

I learnt a great deal about Napoleon in the next few weeks. I raided the history section of the library and read anything about Napoleon that seemed relevant.

The next meeting came round. Fearful, I clasped the paper that had taken me hours to prepare. My name was called. I stood up. There was a little perfunctory clapping. My legs were trembling, my mouth dry. It seemed an age before I got the courage to speak. Then I heard the sound of my own voice and, before long, realised the audience was listening. That brought confidence. In a matter of minutes, it was all over. I sat down, surprised at the clapping. A lively debate followed. Then the ayes and noes were counted. The motion was carried. My first debate was over.

Fortunately, the 'Troubles' had their lighter side.

One afternoon, I was on my way to a lecture at the university. I was walking, and took the shorter way up the hill of Bohermore. The military was everywhere – it was almost impossible to get to the college without meeting some of them. Usually, they took little notice of me. This time, I was stopped at the crossroads by some Free State soldiers.

'Where are you off to?'

'The university.'

'What you got in that bag?'

'Only books.'

'Get them out now.'

I got out a copy of 'Beowulf', and an exercise I had written in Anglo-Saxon script.

'What language is this?' asked the sergeant, looking at the exercise book.

'English.'

'Go on,' he said.

The other soldiers crowded round.

'It's some sort of secret writing,' suggested one. The officer in charge was some distance away. The sergeant took the books to him. He looked at them and laughed. The sergeant came back, gave me my books, and I was allowed to go on.

I especially enjoyed English lectures at the University, though they could hardly be called 'lectures'. The Professor held his students spellbound. Short, and somewhat rotund, he just stood up and talked about whatever aspect of English literature was uppermost in his mind. It might be the diction of Keats one day, the Metaphysical poets another day. Suddenly, we might have a talk on Spenser's *Faerie Queene*. He never had any visible notes. He just wandered backwards and forwards across the lecture-room, talking all the time. At intervals, he caressed a small sandy-grey moustache.

Note-taking by students was almost impossible.

'Read the text for yourselves: read the text for yourselves,' he said again and again. 'Make your own notes.' He never gave essays to write. Occasionally, he gave more formal lectures in Anglo-Saxon. He revelled in the sound, origin and meaning of words.

There was a good deal of grumbling among the students.

'How does he expect us to get through the exams?' said students accustomed to dependence on dictated notes.

For those of us prepared to work, his method of teaching paid off. We were driven to read the texts for ourselves.

The first-year examination came round. Admission to the second year was dependent on passing it. I nearly lost the exam for cheating. We were seated in long parallel rows in the *Aula Maxima*, several subjects being examined simultaneously. I liked the paper and was writing for dear life.

Suddenly, I heard a whisper:

'Frances, Frances.' I ignored this. Again the whisper. 'Frances, Frances, what's a sonnet?' It was Eileen. The whisper became like a refrain. I was being seriously interrupted. Keeping an eye on the Professor, who was invigilating, I bent under a crooked arm and whispered, 'A poem of fourteen lines.'

There was silence for a bit. Then: 'Frances, Frances' came again. 'Who wrote a sonnet?'

Purposely dropping some paper and bending sideways to pick it up, I said, 'Wordsworth.'

The invigilator began to move down the rows. There was complete silence. For a moment, I thought he was coming to me, but he moved on.

When I came back for the afternoon examination, my place had been changed. I felt uneasy, but forgot all about the whispering once I got immersed in the paper. When the papers had been collected, the invigilator called me. Fortunately, he was one who knew me outside the university.

'Do you know why you had a different place this afternoon?'

'Well, not really.'

'You were seen to be talking to someone. As you were writing so much we gave you the benefit of the doubt. Was someone asking you a question?'

'Yes, but I can't say who.'

'We're not going to ask. But let it be a lesson to you. If you're bothered again, just ask if you can have a different place. You nearly forfeited your exam, you know.'

Though I had liked the paper, I was very anxious about the results. Not having written a single essay, I had no standard by which to judge my work.

A few weeks later, my father came in at lunch-time. Lectures had finished.

'Have you been up to the university?' he asked.

'No, why?'

'Well, from what I heard at the club, the results are out.'

I got on my bicycle and rode to the university. In fear and trembling, I went up to the large glass case which contained the examination results. I started at the bottom of the list. I was not among the Passes. I felt a sudden fear. Then, I let my eyes skim the Second-classes. I was not there. The fear increased. Suddenly, amazement overcame me. There was one solitary name in the First Class – mine! I did not feel elation, but guilt. Somehow, I had hoodwinked the examiners!

There was no one else about as it was the vacation. In a daze, I turned my bicycle round. Just as I was about to mount it, I heard my name called. It was the Professor.

'Well, you're a dark horse,' he said. 'The extern liked your wide reading. He said to tell you he'd welcome you at Oxford. There's a compliment for you. You've got a prize, you know.' I didn't know.

'A prize?' I looked at him.

'There's a prize of £7 for the first place in the vernacular.'

Seven pounds was a lot of money! I could afford a new hat. On my way home, I went into the biggest shop in Galway. I chose a dream of a hat, a pale-grey fine straw, mushroom-shaped. It was to be trimmed with a wreath of pink rosebuds.

'I've got a prize,' I told the milliner, who knew me. 'I'll pay as soon as I get it.'

'The hat'll be ready tomorrow, but I'll keep it for you until you get the prize.'

Alas, I didn't get that prize! The Professor had not realised that the official vernacular was not now English, but Irish. The prize went to the student who got the top place in Irish. I had to cancel the order for the hat.

So life went on. From childhood, through adolescence, I never knew anything but war. First, it was the World War in which many of the young men of my generation were killed. Just after the Armistice, 1918, my brother looked up from a newspaper and called to me: 'Frances, do you realise you are one of a million surplus women?'

I didn't realise it then, but time has shown it to be true. I count up my friends of the same age group and find that a very large proportion of them are spinsters.

Almost immediately after the war, the political violence in Ireland erupted. We took this background for granted. Limitations imposed by curfews and the dangers of being out after dark were just a fact of life. Men and women continued to marry: babies were born. But the spectre of death, especially violent death, was never far away.

Memento mori – 'Remember you must die'

Remember man as you pass by,
For as you are, so once was I.
And as I am, so you will be,
Remember man, and pray for me.

That was the epitaph on a granite tombstone, an epitaph which we children often quoted. It was headed by an engraved skull and crossed bones. Death was almost commonplace in my childhood. It was accepted with resignation. Very early in life I became aware of my own mortality. The passing of time filled me with awe. A tall clock stood in the hall of my grandfather's house. Its loud tick-tock, tick-tock seemed to be saying, 'another second gone, another second gone'.

One day, I stood in front of it and watched the long pointed brass second-hand start at twelve, and slowly, but inevitably, creep round again to twelve, accompanied by the inexorable tick-tock.

'A whole minute gone for ever,' I said to myself. 'It can never, never be brought back.'

In the Roman Catholic community, which of course formed the large majority in the West of Ireland, death was treated with much respect. It was most important for someone who had died to be given a good 'wake'.

One Sunday evening, I was passing the cottage of Mr Maloney. I knew he had died that morning. Mrs Maloney was leaning over the half-door. She had on her black shawl over her red petticoat. Her face looked lined and drawn. I went up to the door.

'I'm so sorry to hear of your trouble, Mrs Maloney.'

'Thank you, miss, sure it's the grand man he was. God rest his soul.' She crossed herself. 'It's the lovely corpse he makes. You'll come in? He's all laid out.'

I didn't particularly want 'to view the corpse', as the local saying went, but custom and courtesy overcame my reluctance. I want into the dimly-lit kitchen. A turf fire was burning on the hearth, under a wide chimney opening. A black covered pot with three legs was suspended by a chain from a hook fixed in a brick in the chimney. The smell of baking soda bread came from it. Three loaves were already baked, standing on the deal dresser.

'My son's gone to get the porter,' Mrs Maloney volunteered. 'Maybe he'll get a drop o' the poteen. Sure, it's a good wake we're giving himself.'

My eyes got used to the dimness. I turned towards the corner of the room. On the scrubbed table lay all that remained of Mr Maloney. Four halfpenny candles were burning, one at each corner of the table. Mr Maloney was dressed in his dark grey frieze suit. He had on a stiff white collar and black tie. His hands were folded over a rosary. As I looked at the face, now so peaceful, all lines gone, the eyelids closed, the abundant grey hair so carefully brushed, I wondered why I was so afraid of death.

I turned to Mrs Maloney. 'I didn't know your husband was ill. What happened?'

'By the mercy of God, he had a quiet end. We'd just got back from the early Mass. He sat down in the chair there' – she pointed to the rocking chair by the fire – 'meself was getting a bit of breakfast for the two of us. Suddenly, I heard a sort of moan. I turned, and there was himself all crumpled up like in the chair. "Mick, is yourself all right?" I called. There was never a word out of him.'

'What an awful shock! Where was your son? Was there no one about?'

'Sorra a one. Gerald had gone fishing. But I took me two feet and ran down the road to Pat Curran's. "Get the priest quick," I called. "I think me old man's got death on him." Nora Curran came back with me. We just stood looking at Mick so quiet in the chair. We didn't know what to do.'

'Was Father Dwyer long?'

'No, he came as quick as *his* two feet would carry him.'

'Was he in time?'

'Sure I don't know. But it didn't matter. He gave Mick the last rites.'

'That'll be a consolation to you.'

'Indade, yes. It's what matters. The doctor came soon after, but there wasn't a thing he could do. He was dacent-like – wouldn't take a penny.'

'Is there anything I can do? Have you let your daughters know?'

'Yes, Patrick sent a wire. They'll be here in time for the wake.'

I put sixpence in the plate by the door as I went out. It was, I knew, for the priest. I first realised this when I saw a coffin with a plate on top on a table outside a cottage. Everyone who passed by put a piece of silver on the plate.

'What's the money for?' I asked mother as we paused to put a silver piece on the plate. 'Are they very poor?'

'Yes, but this money is for the priest to say Masses for the soul of the dead man.'

Next day, Mrs O'Brien, who did some cleaning for us, was very late.

'Sure it was at Mick Maloney's wake I was,' she said, assuming that was sufficient explanation.

'Did many go?'

'Oh, indade, there was a big crowd. All night long they played games and told stories. And there was no stint to the drink. It's a good send-off he's having. But it was all fine and dacent-like.'

That there were excesses at wakes was well known. Most of the priests exhorted their flock to decent behaviour.

Late in the evening of that Sunday, I passed the cottage once again on my way back from church. I had an English friend with me. Smoke was pouring from the one chimney. We paused, and glimpsed through the open half-door that the cottage kitchen was packed. Mingled with the laughter and talk was a curious moaning sound.

'What ever's that noise?' asked Phyllis.

'It's the women keening.'

'What on earth's keening?'

'It's the custom round here. A way of mourning. Listen. Can you hear that it has a rhythm? It's not just weeping. It has a pattern of a few notes like intoning.'

'D'ye know,' replied Phyllis, 'it reminds me of the yodelling I heard in Switzerland – only that wasn't mournful.'

'I suppose there is a resemblance. But listen a minute or two. Can you hear the keening rise and fall in volume? When you can't hear the keening so plainly that means that the keening women have thrown their aprons over their heads. Then rocking backwards and forwards, they bury their heads in their laps.'

'How long does it go on for?'

'All the first night after a death, and often at the funeral.'

'How weird. Do the men not keen?'

'No, they play games, tell jokes and get very drunk.'

I first heard keening, not at a wake, but on the station platform in Ballinasloe about 1908. It was an 'American wake'. Rosie O'Reilly was emigrating to America. There she was, seated on a brown tin trunk tied with strong rope. She wore a cheap navy-blue serge suit and a lace blouse. On her head, instead of the customary plaid shawl, was a sailor hat trimmed with roses. As they waited for the train, the many women relatives and friends who came to see her off were keening. This was kept up until the train was out of sight.

Irrespective of class or creed, much respect was paid to the dead on their way to burial. All activity in the streets ceased. Blinds were pulled down in private houses. Shops put up shutters. For a well-known person, shops were completely shuttered. For one less known, a shutter or two sufficed. Anyone meeting a funeral turned and walked a few yards with the procession. It did not matter that the deceased might be quite unknown to the passer-by.

There was usually a hearse, the horse resplendent with black plumes. The coachman's hat had a black crêpe sash round it, the ends reaching nearly to his shoulders. However, it was the custom to take a coffin out of the hearse and carry it. The further the coffin was carried on the shoulders of the male relatives and neighbours, the greater the respect paid to the dead. A fellow student of mine died at the age of eighteen. Her coffin was borne by male students the whole two and a half miles to the cemetery. Teams of four men took it in turn to be bearers.

Protestants condemned the wakes, but had their own ritual of death. The corpse was laid out with new bed-linen, often hoarded for the purpose, and the 'viewing of the corpse' was just as common. A Protestant was always taken to the cemetery in a hearse. Only men walked in the funeral procession though women went to the church service. A widow wore a black mourning veil which reached below her shoulders and completely covered her face. This she wore for six months.

After a Protestant funeral, there was always the funeral tea. Neighbours came and helped with this. A widow would dress in black, but even if her eyes were red from weeping, no one would speak to her of it. The Protestant idea of 'keeping a stiff upper lip' meant that emotion must not be shown in public. In a way, death was eased for Roman Catholics by their beliefs about life after death. The departed spent a time in purgatory before entering heaven. No matter how bad the deceased had been, it was possible to shorten the time spent in purgatory by paying for masses to be offered by the priest for the departed. Such was the popular belief. For the Protestant, the comfort was different. Those who had faith and were 'saved' were 'safe in the arms of Jesus'. What happened after death to the murderer, the drunkard, the wife-beater worried me greatly in my young days.

Death, however, was the great leveller. Faced with the last enemy, Protestant and Catholic found in their common mortality the common humanity that overrode all sectarian differences.

1922–24
Ave atque vale – 'Hail and farewell'

My final examination in 1922 was unusually, and fortunately, in September. My sister came over from England in June and took on the housekeeping for two months. But before that, in May, my study was interrupted.

A telegram came from Ballinasloe: *Come at once. Grandfather very ill.*

Grandfather was 87. 'Come at once' was easier said than done. We had a fairly competent maid. I made her out a menu for a fortnight and packed my case mainly with books. But how was I to get to Ballinasloe? For several weeks, a farce on the railway had been enacted each day. The Dublin train got as far as Athenry, twenty miles from Galway. At Athenry, some police got into the train. As soon as they did, the engine driver and the fireman got out because they refused to carry police. So the train went no further. My father got me a lift to Athenry and I went the rest of the way by train.

Friends of my mother met me and put me up. My grandfather was not expected to live through the night. However, as soon as I arrived he picked up and rallied.

It was quite impossible to get a nurse – they were few and far between and very expensive. His landlady looked after him during the day. Every night, I sat up with him from eight o'clock until eight the next morning. Grandpa slept most of the night. I sat in a fairly comfortable chair, by the turf fire, which I kept well built-up. By the light of two candles, I managed to do a lot of revision for my final examination. Indeed, I had more time for study than at home. So the nights soon passed.

About ten days after I had arrived, I went to bed after breakfast as usual. It seemed that I had hardly got to sleep before I was shaken awake.

'Your grandfather has taken a turn for the worse. You'd better go to him.'

Hastily, I got dressed and went downstairs. Mrs Dawson had a bowl of soup ready for me. 'Now take time to eat this,' she said. 'It may be a long time before you get anything else.'

I had no appetite. I don't like soup, but I appreciated her kindness and common sense, so I ate the bowl of soup. I hurried across the Fair Green, up the hill by the church, down into Dunlo Street. As I knocked on the door of the little Georgian house where grandpa now lived, it was opened by Mrs O'Halahan, his landlady.

'I was on the look-out for you,' she said. 'I think there's death on him.'

I ran up the stairs, shallow for the first two flights, then narrowing and twisting on to the third floor, where grandpa's room was. The door was open. As I went to his bed, I glanced through the window. The hands of the church clock pointed to two; as I looked, the hour struck. Grandpa was lying on his back, quite still, his eyes closed, his grey beard looking as if it had just been trimmed.

I bent over. 'Grandpa, it's Frances.' There was no sign that he heard me. I could see by the slight quiver of his nightshirt that he was still breathing. I sat by him for about an hour. Once, he put out a hand and plucked gently at the bedspread. I put his hand back under the bedclothes. There was no further movement.

Suddenly, I was aware of a change. Grandpa gave a long, low sigh. The church clock struck three. The silence that followed made me believe that he had died. I was not sure. His eyelids were slightly raised: his mouth had fallen slightly open. I felt his feet. They were stone-cold. I put my hand over his heart. Was there a flutter? I got the little mirror out of my handbag, and held it to his mouth. The mirror was clear. So he died, without book or bell or candlestick, a Protestant to the end.

My mother's instructions came back. I stretched out his limbs. I put pennies on his closed eyelids. I tried to tie up his mouth but it was too late. It was already set open. Then I went for the little woman who laid people out. She came back with me, after she had changed into a black blouse and skirt. Her first words were: 'They'll never get the coffin up those stairs. I'll see if Mrs O'Halahan will let me use her spare room below.'

She came back. 'Yes, it'll be all right. Now, you help me carry him down.' What I had to do gave me strength. She wrapped the bottom sheet round my grandfather's body. He was over six feet tall. Between us, she, a little thin woman, and I, a tall thin one, carried my grandfather down the narrow, winding stairs to the spare room. In ten minutes, with the efficiency born of long practice, she had completed her work.

'He's a lovely corpse,' she said. 'Here's his watch. I found it under his pillow.' I took the watch. It had stopped at three o'clock.

That night, tired out, and relieved that it was all over, I slept very soundly. Only in the morning did I know what had happened.

'About eleven o'clock we heard a knocking on the door,' said Mrs Dawson. 'It was the Sinn Feiners. They wanted the car. Mike always takes out a vital part when he leaves, so they couldn't start it. Then they searched for guns. We haven't any. They were just about to search your room. "Must you go in there?" I asked. "There's nothing of any use to you. There's a girl asleep. She's been nursing her grandfather. He died this afternoon. She's tired out." "God rest his soul," they said, and went off.'

Then came the funeral arrangements. There was no time to feel anything. My father could not leave the rest of the family for long. I went to the cemetery and asked for the family grave to be opened. I ordered a coffin and arranged for the body to be taken to the church as soon as possible. It could not remain in the house.

'What are you going to do about black?' Mrs Dawson asked.

'I brought it with me,' I replied. She seemed surprised, but said nothing. I was the only relative.

'I'll walk behind the coffin,' I said.

'Women never walk in funeral processions,' said Mr Dawson. I persisted, so he gave in.

'You're not your mother's daughter for nothing,' he remarked. 'It's just what she would have done.' He and I walked behind the hearse, the only mourners. Down broad Dunlo Street we went on our way to the Presbyterian Church. The blinds went down in every house. A shutter went up on every shop window.

My father got a lift and came for the burial. On the morning of the funeral Mr Dawson said to me: 'Have you checked they've opened the grave?'

'No, but I'll go along.'

I walked the mile to the cemetery. The grave was all ready. Beside it lay the tombstone. On it were my grandmother's name and those of her four sons, three of whom had died in their twenties of tuberculosis.

My grandfather was well-known in the little town. This time a large crowd followed the hearse, all men. I, the only woman, was in a car with my father and the minister. We went at the snail's pace so beloved of the Irish at a funeral. As the funeral approached, again blind after blind went down. Shopkeepers hurried to put up shutters. Passers-by stopped, made the sign of the cross, turned and walked a few yards with the procession.

The coffin was lowered. The gravedigger threw a handful of clay on it. My arm was touched. I turned and saw an elderly beggar, well-known.

'Have you e'er an old waistcoat of the boss's you could let me have?' he said. 'Sure it's the grand man he was.' His question relieved the tension. I could not help laughing.

I was nearing the end of my teacher training. Once again, I was most fortunate in my teacher. He was a Jesuit with a wide experience in education on the continent. He was ahead of his time in educational theory and practice. It was only later that I was to recognise this. For teaching practice, I taught in the little High School. On Saturday morning, I had a class of boys aged about fifteen at the Grammar School. I taught them Irish History, for the National Certificate.

'What was the Composition of Connaught?' appeared on the examination paper. (It was an historic meeting in the sixteenth century.) One boy, interested in geology, but not in history, answered in two words: 'Mainly limestone.'

Part of the examination for the teaching diploma was a demonstration by the student teacher. 'You must have a class of at least twenty for your teaching demonstration,' warned the Education tutor.

This took place at the university. It was observed by several examiners. As I was not able to produce a large enough class from the High School, I borrowed eight boys of the same age group from the Grammar School.

The girls from the High School were quite excited at the prospect of a morning at the university. They had no idea of the purpose of the visit, and were expecting to see interesting things in the science laboratory, such as the jawbone of an ass, or bats in formalin. I heard afterwards that they were very indignant when they found that they were to have a lesson on how to calculate the area of a given triangle.

Three examiners awaited us in the classroom. I had never met the boys from the Grammar School, but they fitted in very well. The children rose to the occasion and responded well. My disappointment was that the examiners departed half-way through the lesson and never saw the cardboard visual aids I had so carefully prepared.

Soon after I obtained my teaching diploma, it was announced that the Headmistress was leaving and the school was likely to close. This caused some consternation among the Protestant parents. A suitably trained teacher who could live on the small salary offered would be hard to find.

Things had quietened down in Ireland. The Free State Government was attempting to function. But several houses of Protestants or Unionists who supported the British were still being burnt down. Rumour had it that ours was on the list. It was probably only a rumour.

My father had not meddled in politics. Local farmers depended on his verterinary services, especially as antibiotics and other modern techniques had not been discovered. However, he wished to marry again. His future wife, though Irish, was established in England. So my younger brothers and sisters were distributed between an uncle and aunt in England. I was left with my father. He decided to auction the contents of the house and move to England.

Clearing-out was a major operation. In the large rambling house with plenty of storage space, there had piled up an enormous collection of what could only be called rubbish. There were piles of the *Veterinary Record* and of the *British Medical Journal* dating back to the beginning of the century. There were trunks and boxes full of dressing-up clothes, including Victorian dresses, bonnets and shawls. They had given us and our friends many hours of pleasure. There were two interesting boxes into which we were allowed to look, but never to play with the contents. One, an oval hat box with the label *Browne Thomas, Grafton Street, Dublin,* contained my grandmother's wedding bonnet, a tiny lace affair trimmed with violets and mauve ribbons. In the other box was a long, thick, dressed plait of my mother's hair. I never knew her anything but grey. This plait was a deep chestnut colour. 'Your grandfather was furious when I had it cut off,' she told me.

In addition to all this junk in the attic there was the miscellaneous collection of books which lined the schoolroom walls. No one wanted any of these things so they were included in the auction.

It was a rush and very hard work to get all this stuff sorted and our personal possessions packed before the auction in the early part of 1923.

The auctioneers arrived early. The senior man said to me: 'Do ye think ye can get the boss to clear out that desk? We want to begin in here.'

I looked at the large mahogany desk. It stood in the middle of the dining-room – a room stripped of everything except what was to be sold. The desk was mountain-high in papers. One touch and all would cascade to the floor.

I found my father.

'The auctioneer wants your desk cleared. They want to begin.'

'I haven't time to do it now. I'm off on an urgent case. It's the last I'll do. See if you can get a big packing case. Put all the stuff in. I'll sort it presently.'

I'd heard that refrain several times during the past weeks. I found a packing case and did a quick rough sorting of the papers. There were bills, old letters, headed writing paper, photographs and some documents relating to my mother's family. In the large drawer I found the Family Bible, the births and deaths of two generations recorded in the front. I filled the case and carefully labelled it. That was the last anyone ever saw of it or its contents.

The auction was packed with people from as far afield as Dublin, attracted by the antique furniture which my mother had collected, often for a song, at auctions. I stood at the window of the attic bedroom and looked down at the crowd. With much pushing and shouting of 'aisy, aisy now', out went the piano. 'Cramer, London' was the name in gold letters above the keyboard. It was walnut wood with a green silk ruching in front. What enjoyment it had given us! Every Sunday evening, in my mother's day, there was hymn singing. 'Shall we gather at the river?', and 'When the roll is called up yonder, I'll be there', were favourites. Most hymns seemed to dwell on some future life. Little was said about the life that was being lived below, except the exhortation, 'Dare to be a Daniel.' Possibly they were a reflection of the early mortality, poverty and hard living of the majority of those who lived in the West of Ireland.

A woman came out with our large black tray. On it were familar cooking utensils. I recognised our big frying pan, and the huge cast-iron griddle. On the big tray, we had tobogganed down the back wooden stairs – a sport usually cut short because of the noise it made.

The woman's right arm was through the handle of the oval pot in which a few evenings before I had boiled twelve lobsters given to my father in place of cash. How I hated the job! But there they were alive, black, and crawling all over each other. It would be cruelty not to boil them as soon as possible. It was nearly ten in the evening. I got the pot mad boiling. Then, holding a lobster with its four claws pinned to its side, I plunged it headfirst into the boiling maelstrom. One little kick. Then it turned red. I hoped it had not felt anything. 'It's the kindest way,' my father said.

A man clutched two framed pictures which had hung in the maid's room. They had come out of *Weldon's Journal*. One showed a man and a woman in an ancient Greek type of dress standing facing each other, very close together. It was called 'Wedded'. When I discovered that the man had paid seven and six for them, I was horrified. 'If people want something, oh sure, they'll pay for it,' said the auctioneer. It did seem a lot of money for two advertisements.

The day ended. The procession of pony traps, donkey carts, wheelbarrows, and the horse-drawn van of a well-known Dublin antique dealer, had at last ceased. The house was stripped. The cows and the donkey had gone the week before. The weeds were rampant in the flower-beds. The grass on the tennis lawn was inches high. The huge brass knocker was tarnished with verdigris from Brasso in the corners. With my father, I went round, pulling up, for the last time, the heavy mahogany shutters on the main windows. He left for England on the night train.

I was tired, but felt nothing. I was only too glad to have come to the end of the sorting-out and clearing-up. I went to friends who had offered to put me up until I could find digs.

About a month after the auction, I was passing our old house. It still stood empty. In a wall, several yards from the house, there was an old letter-box. It was never used. The postman was supposed to deliver letters to the house. Occasionally, a new postman, or a lazy one, put letters in this box. Something made me pause as I passed the house.

I'd better have a look in the outside letter-box, just in case, I thought.

I went inside the grounds. I opened the flap of the letter-box. I expected to find it empty. In it were two letters. One was a bill: the other was addressed to me. Curious, I turned it over. I didn't recognise the educated handwriting. I tore open the envelope and read the letter: *A few of the parents of the High School would like to meet you. They have a proposition to make to you. Can you come to Mrs MacKay's, Ardilaun, on Wednesday, 20 March, at 4.00 pm?'*

It was signed, *John McKenzie*. He was the chairman of the committee that managed the little Girls' High School. I was mystified. What sort of proposition had they in mind? I had no time to consider, for panic seized me. I looked at the letter again. Wednesday, 20 March. Goodness! That was today! I looked at the postmark. It was the tenth of March. The letter had been in the box for over a week. I looked at my watch. It was nearly three o'clock. There was no telephone. There was no way of getting a message to Ardilaun. I cycled the mile back to my digs as quickly as I was able. I dashed upstairs and put on my good coat and skirt and my Sunday hat. I never cycled in my good skirt: it made it shiny. Today there was no choice. The civil war was over. The roads were clear. I got to Ardilaun just on four o'clock and rang the bell. Mrs MacKay opened the door.

'I'm so sorry,' I blurted out. 'Are you expecting me? I only got the letter about an hour ago. It went in the wrong box. I really don't know how to . . .'

Mrs MacKay stopped my flow of apologies. 'No, don't worry. You're here. We did wonder if you'd got the letter. But the committee was meeting anyway. It'll be glad to see you.'

In Mrs MacKay's dining-room were about half a dozen of the parents of the girls at the High School. They were seated at the mahogany table. I knew them all. I started to explain again, why I had not answered the letter. The chairman stopped me with a wave of his hand.

'The main thing is, you're here. Now I'll get straight to the point. Would you be willing to carry on the High School when Miss Richardson goes? We'd see that you had an adequate salary.'

I couldn't say a word. My mind went blank. Then I began to take in the implication of what was being suggested to me.

'Me?' I got out at last. 'Do you mean be the Headmistress?'

'Yes, just that.'

'Oh no, I couldn't. I'm too young!' (I was not yet twenty-three.) 'I couldn't possibly. I've not enough experience.'

'We think you have. If you refuse, the High School must go. Where are the Protestant girls to go? Think it over. We'll give you all the support we can.'

With a mixture of diffidence, because of my age and inexperience, and confidence that teaching was no problem, I took over the school in the autumn term. I was well supported by the parents and things got off to a good start. The parents were relieved that the school was to go on. I tried, with some success, to put into practice the principles so lately given me by the inspired education lecturer at the university.

The Dalton plan was in vogue in America. According to this theory, pupils should work at their own speed; there should be no rewards and no punishments; each pupil must learn for the sake of learning. A wider curriculum, including art and music, was to be introduced. I had written my education study – on which in part my teaching diploma was based – on this theme.

It was an ideal from which I soon departed. My pupils, about twenty-five of them, were of varying social backgrounds and mixed intellectual ability. Before long I was offering incentives to the less-able girls to whom learning for its own sake was not much of a reward.

I was determined, too, with the consent of the managers, to try to break down denominational barriers between Protestant and Catholic.

One day, a Roman Catholic mother came to see me. 'Will you take my two girls?' she asked.

'I'm quite willing, but I don't think your priest will approve.'

'It's my business where the girls go to school, not the priest's,' she retorted.

The girls came. They fitted in well and stayed a month. I was right. The mother was wrong. Under pressure from the priest, they were removed. All the teachers I got in to help me were Roman Catholics, but no problem rose on their account.

I was full of the enthusiasm of the young. In my dreams, I saw the school flourishing, but I wished I did not get so tired. A nagging cough often kept me awake at night.

On Sunday evenings, I often played the harmonium in the Presbyterian Church. It was worked by stiff pedal bellows. The wife of one of the Professors, who attended the Church, noticed that when I began to play, I began to cough. She came to see me. 'My husband would like you to let Dr Devine have a look at your chest. He might be able to do something about that cough of yours.'

Dr Devine was a lecturer in Medicine at the university. He was a very clever young doctor who specialised in diseases of the chest. Sadly, he was soon to die of tetanus, contracted while lifting his son over a stone wall.

I turned up in his consulting room.

'Well, let's see what we can do for you.' He asked me some questions about past illnesses. Then he took out his stethoscope. In those days X-rays were not easily available. The diagnosis of chest troubles largely depended on a doctor's skill with his stethoscope.

'Say ninety-nine,' he said, again and again, as he went over my chest. When he had finished, he made some notes. Then he went and looked out of the window, his back to me. He said nothing for what seemed ages and ages.

He then turned and said: 'I'm afraid you'll have to go away for a bit.'

'Go away! Where? Why?'

'Well, I hear sounds in your lungs I don't like.'

'Do you mean I have consumption?'

'It's in the very early stages. There's nothing some rest won't put right. I'll write to your doctor aunt.'

I left in a daze – no feeling, no emotion. Consumption! How long would I live? I had no illusions. The disease flourished in the mild, damp climate of the West of Ireland. It claimed victims in almost every family. I knew that three of my mother's brothers had died of it.

I forgot the bicycle I had ridden to the university. Over the Salmon Weir Bridge, past the Post Office, round Moon's corner, down Eyre Square, past the station, automatically I took the route with which long years of travelling had made me familiar. Only as I began to feel the pull of the hill, did I realise that I was more than half-way to my old home. Of course, there was no one there now. I turned back. I met a friend of my mother's. Her daughter was a pupil at the school. 'I heard you left school early,' she said. 'Is anything the matter?'

'I've got consumption,' I blurted out.

Her house was nearby. She took me in and gave me something to eat.

So, for the second time in five years, my world seemed to fall apart. But I was an optimist. Three months' rest, the doctor had said. I would be back in three months. Anyway, if I lived to thirty, I'd be really old.

The former Headmistress agreed to take over the school again temporarily. I packed up my books and clothes, and then left them to be stored by my kind landlady.

It was the first day of 1924. I was going over to England to my doctor aunt. She had arranged for three months' treatment in Switzerland. I had just saved enough money to pay for it.

The mail train was due to leave at three o'clock. When I got to the station, it seemed that the entire school had come to see me off. My trunk, packed to capacity, went in the luggage van. I was showered with presents. There was a gift from all of the school of a lovely woollen travelling rug from Connemara. Eileen gave me a big box of chocolates. Margaret, as one would expect, gave me a book. Clara brought a bag of cakes from her mother. 'They're for the journey, mother says.'

'Daddy has sent you these chrysanthemums from his greenhouse.' Shyly, the youngest girl, Molly, handed me a big bunch of golden chrysanthemums. They were lovely, but not the easiest of gifts to manage on a long night journey by train and boat. I thanked them. There was no kissing, no hand shakes, just, 'Thank you all very much. I'll see you at Easter.' I got into an empty carriage. The gifts were piled in. The carriage doors were slammed shut. The whistle sounded. The train began to move.

'Goodbye, goodbye – see you at Easter – happy New Year – safe journey – goodbye – smooth crossing.'

'Goodbye, goodbye.'

Handkerchiefs waved. I looked out of the window until the girls' voices faded in the distance, and waving figures became indistinct. I was alone in the carriage, surrounded by the presents. The bunch of golden chrysanthemums lay on top. I could hardly bear to look at them. The only flowers on my mother's coffin had been golden chrysanthemums. I decided to give them away before I got to Dublin.

The January mist was beginning to come down. The train rounded the bend. The last glimpse of Galway Bay, the water smooth and grey, the Clare hills shrouded in mist, came and went.

'*Ave atque vale*,' I murmured. Prophetically, I had to add, '*Atque in perpetuum, ave atque vale*.'

I did not return to Galway at Easter. My resurrection was to be elsewhere.